Standing in the Circle of Grief

Standing in the Circle of Grief

Prayers and Liturgies for Death and Dying

BLAIR GILMER MEEKS

Abingdon Press
Nashville

STANDING IN THE CIRCLE OF GRIEF
PRAYERS AND LITURGIES FOR DEATH AND DYING

Copyright © 2002 by Abingdon Press

This book is printed on acid-free, recycled, elemental-chlorine–free paper.

Library of Congress Cataloging-in-Publication Data

Meeks, Blair Gilmer.
    Standing in the circle of grief: prayers and liturgies for death and
dying / Blair Gilmer Meeks.
        p.   cm.
    ISBN 0-687-05167-3 (pbk. : alk. paper)
    1. Funeral service.   2. Death—Religious
aspects—Christianity—Prayer-books and devotions—English.   3.
Bereavement—Religious aspects—Christianity—Prayer-books and
devotions—English.   I. Title.
    BV199.F8 .M44   2002
    265'.85—dc21

                                                            2002001538

02 03 04 05 06 07 08 09 10 11—10 9 8 7 6 5 4 3 2 1

MANUFACTURED IN THE UNITED STATES OF AMERICA

For Doug, Bob, Joyce, and John
who with their mother Evelyn †
grew in love and faithfulness
in their circle of grief and hope

In remembrance of Saint Stephen's Day, 1945

Contents

Introduction

Will the Circle
Be Unbroken?

I attended a reception not long ago for a couple who had come to live in our town. I had known this family for years but hadn't seen them in nearly a decade. They greeted me warmly and mentioned the last time we had been together. It wasn't hard to recall that meeting because the occasion was the funeral of their seventeen-year-old daughter, who had died after a long illness. I had watched these parents in the church hall after the funeral as each one stood at the center of a spiraling circle of high school students, teachers, and friends who wanted to surround them with love and embrace them with the comfort they knew would barely touch the overwhelming grief that enveloped them and their community. Now suddenly I was in the circle of grief with them again. "The hardest thing about moving," my friend told me, "was leaving all the people who knew about our daughter."

As a community of faith, we are called to overcome grief's isolation. Those who grieve often feel alone and afraid, but we know that the circle of grief is a bond that connects all human beings. As Mary and Martha longed for Jesus, who came and wept with them at the grave of their brother Lazarus, we long for companionship at the grave of those we love. "What a Friend We Have in Jesus" is often sung at funerals in African American churches, and the words are comforting because we know this friend Jesus as a man of sorrows, acquainted with grief. Until God's final victory over death, there will be weeping at graves everywhere, but we live in the embrace of the community of our friend Jesus. That circle can lift our eyes toward hope.

The circle of grief spans the globe and reaches to ages past. Even when we feel most alone, "we are surrounded by so great a cloud of witnesses." The presence of this circle allows us to "lay aside every weight . . . , looking to Jesus the pioneer and perfecter of our faith, who for the sake of the joy that was set before him endured the cross, disregarding its shame, and has taken his seat at the right hand of the throne of God" (Hebrews 12:1-2). Standing with the risen Jesus, with God our loving Parent, with the Spirit who speaks for us when we cannot speak, and with the faithful who have gone before, we can endure our sorrow "for the sake of the joy" that comes with the morning. Through the prayers of the church, the circle of grief can become a circle of blessing.

The prayers in this book are written for the community to pray together with those in grief. They may be used with the bereaved at the time of death, they may be included in funeral or memorial services, or they may become a part of worship services at church or in the home throughout the year. We know that grieving cannot be scheduled and rarely concludes after the funeral service. There is often a return of deep sorrow at particular times of the year: Christmas, an anniversary, a birthday. We know also that there are singular aspects to grief—no one experiences a death in quite the same way as anyone else. There are deaths that come gently as to someone prepared to die after a good, long life, and there are deaths that knock us to the ground with their untimeliness—the death of a child, the suicide of someone we love. Sometimes we pray in anguish, searching the Scriptures for words to shout in anger or cry in despair. Sometimes we pray in silence, relying on the Spirit to intercede for us with "sighs too deep for words" (Romans 8:26).

For all occasions of grief, beginning with the funeral, our prayers acknowledge the reality of death and the pain of being parted by death from someone we love. Prayers in our community of faith, however, acknowledge a greater reality: the certainty that God has raised Jesus from the dead and that God's power over death will bring life to all. "In a moment, in the twinkling of an eye. . . . For the trumpet will sound, and the dead will be raised imperishable, and we will be changed" (1 Corinthians 15:52). If, as Paul says, we believe that death will be "swallowed up in victory" (v. 54), then God's name will be praised at every funeral. We will preach and pray in the glorious promise of the resurrection.

The prayers here for the most part follow traditional prayer forms—collects, litanies, and blessings—and they use familiar images from Scripture. The echoes of biblical and traditional prayers will help connect us with the generations of witnesses. But prayers are included for various situations that might not be found in traditional prayer books, and they are intended to resonate with our times as well as with our heritage of faith. Through lives of prayer, we witness to God's power over death. We join with all the saints, present with us in our acts of prayer and praise, in an unbroken circle of those who wait for God's promised victory over the last enemy.

I
Prayers with a Bereaved Family

These prayers and scriptures are suitable for use with those present at the death of a loved one or on the first pastoral visit to the home or hospital after a death.

—m—

Surrounding the Deathbed with Prayer

Pastor or Pastoral Visitor:
In this moment of sorrow we can be assured that God is with us. God hears the cries of those who suffer and blesses those who mourn. Let us pray in silence.

(Silence)

Jesus said to Martha, when he came to her after her brother's death: "I am the resurrection and the life. Those who believe in me, even though they die, will live" (John 11:25).

Let us join hands now and pray for our *[sister/brother Name]*, who has died.

Gracious God, receive your servant *[Name]*,
for *[she/he]* returns to you.
May *[she/he]* know your ceaseless care
and remain in the joy of your peace.
We thank you for the life of *[Name]*,
for the work that *[she/he]* did among us,
for the joys and sorrows of a lifetime,
and for the love that we shared.
We thank you that for *[Name]* death is past and pain has
    ended;
we ask that *[she/he]* may rest in the comfort of your arms.
Grant to those who are bereaved faith and strength
that they may meet the days to come with hope,
in thankful remembrance of your great mercy,
and in confidence that they will join again
with those they love in your eternal home.
In the name of Jesus, our Resurrection and our Life.
    Amen.

Our Father, who art in heaven,
   hallowed be thy name.
Thy kingdom come,
   thy will be done on earth as it is in heaven.
Give us this day our daily bread.
And forgive us our trespasses,
   as we forgive those who trespass against us.
And lead us not into temptation,
   but deliver us from evil.
For thine is the kingdom, and the power, and the glory,
   forever. Amen.

(The pastor may read the following verses of Scripture.)

> Blessed be the God and Father of our Lord Jesus Christ,
> the Father of mercies and the God of all consolation, who
> consoles us in all our affliction, so that we may be able to
> console those who are in any affliction with the consola-
> tion with which we ourselves are consoled by God. For
> just as the sufferings of Christ are abundant for us, so
> also our consolation is abundant through Christ. . . . Our
> hope for you is unshaken; for we know that as you share
> in our sufferings, so also you share in our consolation.
> (2 Corinthians 1:3-5, 7)

> As a mother comforts her child, so I will comfort you.
> (Isaiah 66:13*a*)

Blessing:
May the peace of God,
which surpasses all understanding,
guard our hearts and minds in Christ Jesus.
May the grace of the Lord Jesus Christ,
the love of God,
and the communion of the Holy Spirit
be with all of you. Amen.
   (adapted from Philippians 4:7; 2 Corinthians 13:13)

Prayers for Guidance

Your steadfast love, O LORD, extends to the heavens,
  your faithfulness to the clouds.
Your righteousness is like the mighty mountains,
  your judgments are like the great deep;
  you save humans and animals alike, O LORD.
How precious is your steadfast love, O God!
  All people may take refuge in the shadow of your
    wings.
They feast on the abundance of your house,
  and you give them drink from the river of your
    delights.
For with you is the fountain of life;
  in your light we see light.
O continue your steadfast love to those who know you,
  and your salvation to the upright of heart!
                                        (Psalm 36:5-10)

God of comfort,
you heal the brokenhearted:
Guide us to seek you in our need and put our trust in
  you.
God of wisdom,
you give us your word and you know our thoughts:
Guide us in the days ahead that we may act according to
  your will.
God of life,
by his death your Son took away the sting of death
so that we may one day be raised in his likeness:
Guide us in our sorrow to praise the victory that awaits
  us.
God of hope,
you have made a place for us and those we love:
Guide us to the river of life that flows by your glorious
  home.

God of grace,
you offer shelter to the living and the dead:
Guide us that we may sing for joy in the shadow of your
wings.
In the name of Jesus. Amen.

Loving God,
you are the Father and Mother of all who dwell on earth
and in heaven.
Look kindly on your children who are overcome by loss
and sorrow.
In our doubt, give us grace to trust, though we do not
understand.
In our loneliness, may we remember [Name] in love,
assured that [she/he] is in your keeping until the dawn of
your new day.
In our fear, bless us with your presence
and give us courage for the days to come.
In our confusion, direct our thoughts and decisions
that we may be guided by your wisdom in all we do.
In our weakness, uphold us that we may believe the good
news
and wait on your tender mercies, new every morning.
In our grief, give us the comfort of your Spirit
and surround us with the love of others
who embrace us in your name.
In our need, be our rest, our hope, our life,
for we pray in the name of Jesus, our beginning and our
end. Amen.

Prayers for Comfort

"Amen! Blessing and glory and wisdom
  and thanksgiving and honor
  and power and might
  be to our God forever and ever! Amen." . . .
"For this reason they are before the throne of God,
  and worship him day and night within his temple,
  and the one who is seated on the throne will shelter
    them.
They will hunger no more, and thirst no more;
  the sun will not strike them,
  nor any scorching heat;
  for the Lamb at the center of the throne will be their
    shepherd,
  and he will guide them to springs of the water of life,
  and God will wipe away every tear from their eyes."
                              (Revelation 7:12, 15-17)

God our Shepherd,
you have promised to wipe away our tears
and guide us to the waters of life.
Sustain us now, for we are overcome with grief.
Give us grace to wait on your goodness,
to expect an end to our hunger and longing,
for we will once again join hands with those we love.
Grant us a place in the home you have prepared
that we may find peace in the shelter of your fold.
Teach us new songs of praise
that we may join the choir before your throne,
singing your glory and praising your power,
for you have raised Jesus to reign at your right hand.
In his name we pray. Amen.

Gracious God, Father of all mercies, Mother of
   consolation,
hear us in our distress.
You, O God, are always near to us;
you are our rock in times of need.
Help us in our shock and grief.
Make us ready to listen quietly to your word.
Disperse our fears and ease our loneliness.
Assure us in your mercy
that our loved one *[Name]* is always in your care.
Lift us from the shadow of death
that we may see the light of your face
and know the tender mercy of your embrace.
Give us grace to live in hope of that day
when we will all be raised like Jesus,
your Son, our Savior, in whose name we pray. Amen.

Prayers for the Strengthening of Faith

But we do not want you to be uninformed, brothers and sisters, about those who have died, so that you may not grieve as others do who have no hope. For since we believe that Jesus died and rose again, even so, through Jesus, God will bring with him those who have died.

(1 Thessalonians 4:13-14)

God our refuge and strength,
you know what we need before we ask.
Come to us in our weakness and grief;
be our wisdom in confusion and doubt.
Be gracious to us and embrace us
that we may not be overwhelmed by our loss.
Surround us with your community of love;
carry us by the faith we claim as Christ's body.
Give us courage even in the face of death
to proclaim your gift of life
and praise your goodness to those who walk with you.
In the name of Jesus, risen and glorified. Amen.

Holy God,
through your creative love you gave us birth,
and by your redeeming love
you have made us a new creation.
Teach us to lean on your love alone.
Beloved Jesus,
you were born like us; you died like us;
and as you were raised, we will be raised from death.
Teach us to walk with you toward newness of life.
Spirit of peace, Comforter,
you came as our companion; you make us whole.
Teach us to stand, filled with your power,

firm in our faith, and blessed with your hope.
In the name of Jesus,
who reigns with God and the Holy Spirit,
now and forever. Amen.

> May the God of hope fill you with all joy and peace in
> believing, so that you may abound in hope by the power
> of the Holy Spirit.
>
> (Romans 15:13)

II

Prayers and Readings for a Vigil or Visitation

On the evening before a funeral, family and close friends of the deceased may gather at the funeral home, in the church parlor, or in a home. In some traditions a wake or vigil is planned for this gathering with prayers, scripture readings, and storytelling. Even if there is no precedent for such a service, a time of prayer and remembering is always appropriate, especially at the beginning or end of the evening. Pastors or family members can use the following prayers and readings as a way to remember the deceased and remind the mourners of God's compassion and God's promise of life in Jesus Christ.

—⟘⟘—

Greeting

Leader:
Dear friends,
at this time of death and parting,
we know that God is with us and calls us by our name.
Let us pray in silence as we remember *[Name]*.

(Silence)

God of joy and sorrow,
we are your children; we live and die in your care:
We trust to you now the care of our *[sister/brother, Name]*,
who has never left the reach of your love.
Comfort us in our grief and strengthen our faith.
Bless us with memories of our life with *[Name]*
and remind us of the joy of *[her/his]* presence.
We thank you for your promise of life that endures,
and for your loving arms that enfold all your children
    now and forever.
In Jesus' name. Amen.

Let us pray together the prayer Jesus taught us:

(The Lord's Prayer)

The Word of God

(The Old Testament and Gospel readings may be read by two or more readers, and the psalm antiphonally by groups on either side of the room.)

Isaiah 43:1*d*-3*a*, 5-7

Do not fear, for I have redeemed you;
    I have called you by name, you are mine.
When you pass through the waters, I will be with you;

and through the rivers, they shall not overwhelm you;
when you walk through fire you shall not be burned,
and the flame shall not consume you.
For I am the LORD your God,
the Holy One of Israel, your Savior.
Do not fear, for I am with you;
I will bring your offspring from the east,
and from the west I will gather you;
I will say to the north, "Give them up,"
and to the south, "Do not withhold;
bring my sons from far away
and my daughters from the end of the earth—
everyone who is called by my name,
whom I created for my glory,
whom I formed and made."

Psalm 121 (adapted)

I lift up my eyes to the hills—
from where will my help come?
My help comes from the LORD,
who made heaven and earth.
[The LORD] will not let your foot be moved;
[the One] who keeps you will not slumber.
[The One] **who keeps Israel**
will neither slumber nor sleep.
The LORD is your keeper;
the LORD is your shade at your right hand.
The sun shall not strike you by day,
nor the moon by night.
The LORD will keep you from all evil . . .
will keep your life.
The LORD will keep
your going out and your coming in
from this time on and forevermore.

(Hymn: "O God Our Help in Ages Past" [Psalm 90])

John 14:1-7, 18-20

"Do not let your hearts be troubled. Believe in God, believe also in me. In my Father's house there are many dwelling places. If it were not so, would I have told you that I go to prepare a place for you? And if I go and prepare a place for you, I will come again and will take you to myself, so that where I am, there you may be also. And you know the way to the place where I am going."

Thomas said to him, "Lord, we do not know where you are going. How can we know the way?"

Jesus said to him, "I am the way, and the truth, and the life. No one comes to the Father except through me. . . .

"I will not leave you orphaned; I am coming to you. In a little while the world will no longer see me, but you will see me; because I live, you also will live. On that day you will know that I am in my Father, and you in me, and I in you."

Leader:
God, you loved the world so much that you sent your
    Son,
who lived like us, died like us, and became the first to rise
    again.
Give us grace to remember that in our baptism we share
    his death, and we will also rise like him.
Guide us safely through the waters
and bring us to our home with you and your Son, Jesus
    Christ. Amen.

Acts of Peace and Reconciliation

Leader:
I invite you now to remember God's mercy to all who come together to make peace. God calls us to be reconciled with each other and live in love that others may see God's grace. We know that no one lives free from discord and conflict. We sometimes find ourselves at cross purposes with friends or family members and later wish for an opportunity to make amends. When someone we love dies, we may regret that we never asked forgiveness for something we said or did, or we may regret that we never received an apology we had hoped for. Now is the time to lay those burdens before God.

Let us pray together:

God of mercy,
you know the secrets of our hearts,
and you are always ready to listen.
Help us to lay down every regret,
every word we would like to take back,
every missed chance to say "I'm sorry."
Help us to let go our disappointments
and to accept your words of peace.
Guide our thoughts to your love
that surrounds us and all those we hold dear.
Hear us as we pray.

(Silent prayers)

Leader:
God, you are faithful and just;
you forgive and cleanse us.
Bathe us with your living waters
that we may have harmony with each other,

peace within our hearts, and hope for your future.
In Jesus' name. Amen.

The risen Christ stood among his disciples and said,
"Peace be with you." Let us now exchange greetings and
signs of peace.

(*The participants greet each other with handclasps or embraces,
exchanging greetings such as "The peace of Christ be with
you."*)

(*Hymn: "Blest Be the Tie That Binds"*)

Naming

Leader:
Our [brother/sister Name] was blessed and named as a
child of God at [his/her] baptism. [He/She] was a blessing
in our lives, and we will continue to enjoy the memories
of our time together. All of you here tonight, and especially the family and friends who knew [her/him] best, can
tell us stories to help us remember [Name's] joys and con-
tributions to our lives as well as the mishaps and sur-
prises we encountered together. Some of you have
prepared a story or reading that will help us name
[her/him] as a person whose life affected us, someone we
will miss and who we know remains always in God's
care. I invite you to share your reflections with us now.

(*The family may choose several persons to speak for them about
a particular aspect of the deceased person's life, and others may
join the storytelling as time permits. The leader closes by reading a favorite Bible passage of the deceased and inviting all to
sing a well-loved hymn.*)

Closing Prayer

Leader:
God, you are all compassion;
your Son Jesus left his rightful place with you
to become one of us, subject to human weakness,
blessed with human joy, and acquainted with grief.
Hear us now in our sadness and loneliness.
Give us courage to meet the days ahead
sure of your presence, secure in your promises,
trusting *[Name]* to your faithful care.
Grant us grace to know the comfort of family and friends,
Come to us with your word of hope,
that we may know the love of this same Jesus,
who died and rose again and reigns exalted
with you and the Holy Spirit,
ready to welcome us all into your new creation.
In his name we pray. Amen.

III

Prayers for Particular Occasions of Death

Each person's death carries particular meaning and a singular grief. We are often unable to express the depth of our sorrow over a friend who dies in middle age with so much left to give and receive. We face the news of a suicide with sadness and fear, sometimes even with a sense of failure. And the death of a child is overwhelming because, in addition to deep grief, it brings with it a sense that the orderliness of life has been overturned. The prayers in this section have been written out of the experience of deaths that challenged my own understanding and caused me to search for the words to pray at a funeral or memorial service.

—∿∿—

After Suicide

For I am convinced that neither death, nor life, nor angels, nor rulers, nor things present, nor things to come, nor powers, nor height, nor depth, nor anything else in all creation, will be able to separate us from the love of God in Christ Jesus our Lord.

(Romans 8:38-39)

God of mercy,
your Son Jesus became like us
and lived like us through trouble and sorrow,
shock and confusion:
Grant us grace to know his compassion,
to carry with us his sure sense of our every need.
Give us courage to walk with Jesus, who bears our burdens
and knows how fragile our endurance is.
When we are angry,
help us know we have not been forsaken.
When we are unforgiving,
remind us that you forgive and wash away the hurt.
When we cannot be comforted,
let us feel your tears on us like rain from heaven.
When we think we have failed,
remind us that we are bearers of your steadfast love.
When we are fearful and unsure,
show us the shelter of your wings that stretch beyond
    our sight.
Gather in your embrace all who long for your rest:
those in despair, in pain, in fear,
and those who cause our hearts to ache.
Reunite us in the home you have prepared with
    Jesus your Son,
who came to those with deepest needs
and reaches out to bring all people to your joy.
In his name we pray. Amen.

After a Preventable Death

"LORD, let me know my end,
  and what is the measure of my days;
  let me know how fleeting my life is. . . .
"And now, O Lord, what do I wait for?
  My hope is in you. . . .
"Hear my prayer, O LORD,
  and give ear to my cry;
  do not hold your peace at my tears.
For I am your passing guest. "
                                   (Psalm 39:4, 7, 12*a*)

God, our refuge and strength in sorrow,
you know the workings of our minds;
you understand all mysteries.
Give us grace to lay our confusion and protest before you.
Help us to let go of our anger and frustration
at grief that might have been postponed.
Heal our troubled hearts and grant us peace.

God, we know that death is never your will,
and yet you are ever ready to receive us.
Grant us peace.
God, we know you are dismayed when death prevails,
and still you open wide the door to life.
Grant us peace.
God, we know that you will end death's unjust hold;
now keep us from the shadow of despair.
Grant us peace.

God, in your mercy,
lift our eyes to Jesus,
whose wrongful death brought life and hope
because he is your risen Son
and reigns with you in peace and joy now and forever.
  Amen.

After an Event in Which Many People Died

Comfort, O comfort my people,
   says your God.
Speak tenderly to Jerusalem,
   and cry to her. . . .
The LORD is the everlasting God,
   the Creator of the ends of the earth.
[The LORD] does not faint or grow weary;
   [The LORD's] understanding is unsearchable.
[The LORD] gives power to the faint,
   and strengthens the powerless.
Even youths will faint and be weary,
   and the young will fall exhausted;
but those who wait for the LORD shall renew
     their strength,
   they shall mount up with wings like eagles,
they shall run and not be weary,
   they shall walk and not faint.
          (Isaiah 40:1-2*a*, 28*b*-31 adapted)

God of heaven and earth,
you know the sound a sparrow makes
when it falls to the ground.
Hear now our voices joined in quiet outrage.
We are thunderstruck, and we cannot find words.
Send your Spirit to speak for us, O God,
to plead our case before you
and release the anguish of our hearts.

God of all consolation,
we cry for peace, and there is none in our hearts.
Send your river of life flowing through us
to cleanse the wounds of our sorrow
and still the turmoil of our minds.

We cry against the flagrant waste of lives,
promises that will not be kept,
friendships lost, the love of family left ungratified.
Our cries protest the deaths
that rob the living and the dead of precious time
and plunge us into depths of grief and pain.
Because we cannot understand,
show us your peace that surpasses understanding.

God of life,
your anger sears the mountains
and strikes terror in those who spurn your will:
Open our eyes to your presence and let us see
that death is always counter to your word.
Show us your streams that rush with living water,
your mindful watch in every struggle against death.
Give us grace to know your gift of Jesus,
our companion through death's night,
and our guide to your new day's glory.
Fill us with your Spirit's breath of life
and lift us to you in our need
that we may know your sorrow, deep as our own,
and hear your word of hope.
In Jesus' name. Amen.

At the Cessation of Life Support

The one who raised the Lord Jesus will raise us also with Jesus, and will bring us with you into his presence. Yes, everything is for your sake, so that grace, as it extends to more and more people, may increase thanksgiving, to the glory of God.

(2 Corinthians 4:14-15)

(A circle may be formed around the bed by joining hands, including, if allowed, the person who is losing artificial life support.)

Gracious God,
you have supported us through all our days;
you are our breath, the source of all our needs.
Be with us now, Author of life,
and keep our loved one *[Name]* in your tender care.
Comfort us and grant us peace.
Give us courage to release *[Name]* from our hands,
from all our efforts to bring *[him/her]* back to us in health.
God, our healer, embrace *[Name]* now
that *[she/he]* may rest in your peace,
and make us whole again in that new day
when we will all join hands and sing in joy with you.
In the name of Jesus, risen and glorified; Alleluia! Amen.

(The sign of the cross may be made over the person who is losing life support, or on the person's forehead; other gestures of farewell may be given.)

᷎

After the Death of a Divorced Spouse

(For a pastoral visit or a gathering of friends and family.)

> I believe that I shall see the goodness of the LORD
>   in the land of the living.
> Wait for the LORD;
>   be strong, and let your heart take courage;
>   wait for the LORD!
>
> (Psalm 27:13-14)

God of mercy,
your Son Jesus made us his sisters and brothers
and promised us rooms in your new household.
Give us grace to be at home this day surrounded by
    your love.
Help us to lay down every regret
and let go our disappointments.
Release us from the hold of painful memories,
guide us to recall your blessings,
and lead us to accept your words of peace.
Hear us as we pray.

(Silent prayers)

God, you are just and forgiving.
Teach us your forgiveness.
We bring to you our troubled hearts,
our thoughts that run from grief to hurt,
and ask for the still waters of your peace.

(Silent prayers)

God, you hold us all in life and death.
Strengthen our faith that we may without fear

give ourselves and those who have died
to your enduring love.
Give rest to *[Name]* and grant *[him/her]* your peace.
Free us and cleanse us with your healing balm,
that we may have harmony with each other
and live with peaceful hearts in your life-giving hope.
In Jesus' name. Amen.

&

After the Death of an Abusive Parent

For all who are led by the Spirit of God are children of
God. For you did not receive a spirit of slavery to fall
back into fear, but you have received a spirit of adoption.
When we cry, "Abba! Father!" it is that very Spirit bearing witness with our spirit that we are children of God,
and if children, then heirs, heirs of God and joint heirs
with Christ—if, in fact, we suffer with him so that we
may also be glorified with him.

(Romans 8:14-17)

Merciful God,
your love never ends;
by your love we judge all other loves
and find them wanting.
Heal us from all harm and abuse;
wash our wounds with living water,
that we may know from your strong hands
a father's true compassion, a mother's tender care.
As your Son at his death forgave the ones who did
    him harm,
teach us the forgiveness that calms our troubled minds.
Free us from the bonds of fear and anger,
that we may also release to you our *[father/mother Name]*,

whose death gives rise to painful memory
and brings us unexpected grief.
May our tears flow freely,
and join with those you shed for all who wait on your
    justice.
Chase away the clouds of night
and make our hearts open to your grace,
that we may give you charge of *[Name]* in death
and live in peace, safeguarded by your love.
In the name of Jesus, our Resurrection and our Life,
    Amen.

After a Miscarriage

Hannah prayed and said,
"My heart exults in the LORD;
my strength is exalted in my God. . . .
There is no Holy One like the LORD,
    no one besides you;
    there is no Rock like our God."
                    (1 Samuel 2:1*a*, 2)

God, our hope,
you know our sorrow;
you are all compassion.
Lead us to your mercy seat
and hear us in our distress.
As Hannah poured out her soul before you in grief,
we ask that you hear your servants *[Name]* and *[Name]*;
guide their thoughts and give them comfort in your care.
Heal *[Name]* from all that she has suffered in mind and
    body,
and show your lovingkindness to her;
for, in this brief time of expectation,

she gave of all she had to nourish your gift of life within her,
as you, O God, surround and nurture us from our
    beginning.
Give to [Name] and [Name] signs of your presence;
relieve them from anxiety, confusion, and uncertainty,
and free them from all fear.
Guide us to embrace them in your love,
that they may not bear their loss alone.
Grant them grace to wait on your goodness
and see what Hannah saw: the weak girded with strength,
the needy lifted up, and life brought out of death.
We pray in the name of Jesus,
whose reign will bring to fullness all our hopes. Amen.

After an Abortion

Jesus said to them, "I am the bread of life. Whoever
comes to me will never be hungry, and whoever believes
in me will never be thirsty. . . . Everything that the Father
gives me will come to me, and anyone who comes to me
I will never drive away; for I have come down from
heaven, not to do my own will, but the will of him who
sent me. . . . This is indeed the will of my Father, that all
who see the Son and believe in him may have eternal life;
and I will raise them up on the last day."

(John 6:35, 37-40)

Gracious God,
you know the needs and desires of our hearts;
when we do not know how to pray as we ought,
your Spirit intercedes for us.
Speak words of hope for your servant(s) [Name(s)]
that she [they] may know the mercies of your love.
Grant [Name] the protection of your strong arms
that she may find rest and healing.

Let her know the love of others
who care for her in your name,
and may their care ease her heartache and fears.
Give strength to *[Name(s)]*
that she *[they]* may go forward in your love
and feel the light of your face shining on her *[them]*.
Merciful God, all creation is in your care;
your love makes all things new;
now give to *[Name(s)]* your peace
that she *[they]* may be open to your call and live in grace.
Unite us in your love and lead us to the river of life
that flows from your throne and bathes us in your mercy.
In Jesus' name. Amen.

For a Stillborn Infant

But now thus says the LORD,
  he who created you, O Jacob,
  he who formed you, O Israel:
Do not fear, for I have redeemed you;
  I have called you by name, you are mine.
                 (Isaiah 43:1)

(The parents may hold and name the child. The pastor may bless and anoint the child.)

Loving God, you have made us your children;
you are our loving Parent.
Now bless your child *[Name]*,
whom we hold before you in grief and love.
Grant that *[he/she]*, whom we have named and given to
    your care,
may know your voice and hear you call *[his/her]* name.
Surround *[him/her]* with your love

as *[he/she]* was surrounded by *[his/her]* mother's womb.
Prepare for *[him/her]* a place in your home
as *[his/her]* parents have prepared their home in hope
    and expectation.
Bless *[mother's Name]* and heal her;
fill her with your love
that she may know your presence in her emptiness and
    loss.
Bless *[father's Name]* and comfort him;
help him stand against the shock of grief
and hold him fast in your love.
Bless *[grandparents' Names]* and all those who mourn with
    this family.
All our bright dreams have vanished,
and our deep grief is more than we can bear.
Have mercy on us and on this precious child;
cherish *[him/her]* always as we hold *[him/her]* in our hearts.
Keep our love for each other steadfast
and bound in love for you.
Make us stronger every day,
that we may know again your gift of life and joy,
sealed for us by Jesus' death and resurrection.
In his name we pray. Amen.

After the Death of a Child

Jesus . . . said to them, "Let the little children come to me;
do not stop them; for it is to such as these that the kingdom of God belongs."

(Mark 10:14)

Compassionate God,
you have promised to be with those who gather in your
   name.
Now hear this community of mourners
as we surround the parents, *[Name]* and *[Name]*,
whose beloved child has died.
Hear our cries;
break through our wall of grief and fear
and give us strength to cling to Jesus' love that knows
   no bounds.
Dear God, you grieved for your beloved Son,
and still you grieve for your dying children everywhere.
Now receive the tears of these parents
who loved their child *[Name]* more than anyone but
   you can know,
and love *[her/him]* still with a love that reaches to your
   glorious home,
where they will one day hold *[her/him]* in their arms
   again.
Comfort them and assure them that you are ready to
   receive *[Name]*
and that you will embrace this child and keep *[her/him]* in
   your care.
As your Son Jesus took the children in his arms and
   blessed them,
bless *[Name]* and bless our memories of *[her/him]*,
that we may remember the laughter and tears of *[her/his]*
   short life,

the pleasures of loving and being loved by such a child.
Give us grace to find meaning and hope in this child's life,
precious to you and to all who knew *[her/him]*,
and to give you thanks, even as we protest death's
    unjust hand.
We pray in the name of Jesus, for *[Name]* is a lamb of
    Jesus' flock,
and Jesus will carry *[her/him]* to the fold of life. Amen.

                       ⤳

After the Death of a Teenager

Have you not known? Have you not heard?
The LORD is the everlasting God,
    the Creator of the ends of the earth. . . .
Even youths will faint and be weary,
    and the young will fall exhausted;
but those who wait for the LORD
    shall renew their strength,
        they shall mount up with wings like eagles,
they shall run and not be weary,
    they shall walk and not faint.
                  (Isaiah 40:28*a b*, 30-31)

Everlasting God, we belong to the One whose gift is life;
by our praise and thanksgiving we witness against the
    power of death
and live in your blessing from generation to generation.
Have mercy on us in our sorrow.
Grace us with your hope and comfort,
and let us find even in our heartache
the words to give you thanks for *[Name's]* young life,
to praise you for the blessings of your Spirit
that flowed through *[him/her]* and touched *[her/his]*
    friends and family.

Hear *[Name's]* parents, *[Names]*,
and hold them, for their loss is beyond measure.
Give comfort to *[Names of grandparents]*,
who have lost a precious *[granddaughter/grandson]*
and also know the anguish of a child who mourns.
Give courage and hope to *[Names of sibling(s)]*;
let *[him/her/them]* feel your presence and grow stronger.
Bless *[Name's]* friends, who are acquainted too soon with
    grief;
help them grow in faith and never lose their trust in you.
Show us in your mercy that Jesus hears us and knows our
    despair,
that he cries with us in our anger and pain and will heal
    us.
Give us strength to walk toward the light of your face,
trusting, though we do not understand,
that nothing separates us from your love.
In the name of Jesus your Son, who died for us and
    rose again;
in the name of Jesus, our friend, who waits to welcome
    [Name]
and gives us grace to wait in hope for God's new
    morning. Amen.

After a Death in Midlife

We do not live to ourselves, and we do not die to ourselves. If we live, we live to the Lord, and if we die, we die to the Lord; so then, whether we live or whether we die, we are the Lord's. For to this end Christ died and lived again, so that he might be Lord of both the dead and the living.

(Romans 14:7-9)

O God, who by the glorious resurrection of your Son
assured that one day death will be no more
and crying will cease,
come to us and give us peace.
Help us in our sorrow and struggle,
for we do not understand why *[Name]*
should suffer and die in the midst of life,
why we should lose *[her/his]* good service
and the blessings of *[her/his]* presence in all we did
    together.
Bless *[her/his]* family and friends *[especially Names]*.
and be present with them in their loneliness and grief.
We thank you for your merciful kindness to all who are
    in pain,
and for your healing balm that makes the wounded
    whole.
Take away our fear, and let us say before our enemy
    death:
"You have done your worst, nevertheless God will
    prevail."
Give us faith, even in sorrow,
to see your victory through Jesus' death and resurrection,
so that in confidence we may continue the work you give
    us
until, by your call, we are reunited with those we love.

In the name of Jesus,
who reigns with you and the Holy Spirit,
one God now and forever. Amen.

❧

After a Death at the End of a Long Life

Not that I have already . . . reached the goal; but I press
on to make it my own, because Christ Jesus has made me
his own. . . . but this one thing I do: forgetting what lies
behind and straining forward to what lies ahead, I press
on toward the goal for the prize of the heavenly call of
God in Christ Jesus. . . . But our citizenship is in heaven,
and it is from there that we are expecting a Savior, the
Lord Jesus Christ.

(Philippians 3:12-14, 20)

God of grace and glory,
you have set a high calling before us
and made us citizens of Jesus' reign.
Give us grace to see in the life of our *[sister/brother Name]*
the fullness of your blessing,
the abundance and the beauty of your gifts.
We give you thanks for *[Name's]* long life,
rich in grace and filled with your favor,
and for *[his/her]* presence and work in this community.
Give us comfort in our memories of laughter and tears,
of giving and receiving, of cares and joys,
of loving and being loved.
Comfort those who mourn, especially *[Names]*,
and bless them, for they have loved faithfully
and now long for their loved one's company.
Give them peace in knowing that *[Name]* was washed in
    baptism,

received the Holy Spirit, and now is welcomed by your
   saints.
We thank you, God, that *[Name]* was nourished at your
   table here
and that you have set a place for *[him/her]* at the table in
   your glorious home.
Bless and keep us for that morning when the stars begin
   to fall,
when we will hear the trumpet sound
and stand before you, joining with your hosts above
in the eternal song of praise to you our Creator,
to Jesus Christ, risen and glorified,
and to the Holy Spirit, one God now and forever. Amen.

IV

Prayers and Readings for Funerals and Other Memorial Services

In our congregational prayer at funerals and other services of remembrance, we praise God who creates life and conquers death. We recognize the pain of being parted from loved ones by death, but we give thanks for the promised resurrection and for God's comforting and sustaining presence.

How do we sing a song of praise in the alien land of grief? We are given models in the psalms of prayers that express intense anger and deep sadness and yet recognize the splendor of God's works. Throughout Scripture we have the testimony of witnesses to God's power for life, and we have the story of Jesus, who willingly became subject to death and was raised to stand again among his friends, eating and drinking with those who knew him. We have Jesus' words that he would rise again and go to his Father's house in order to prepare a place for us (John 14:1-6).

Our task as leaders of prayer for the grieving is not only to help them find words for the despair and anger but also to speak words of hope and praise together with them. It is even possible for us who are members of Christ's body to pray in the place of those who cannot yet pray for themselves. Those most closely touched by grief need the embrace of the faith community, who suffers with them, acknowledges the pain and injustice of death, and holds them up in their distress. They also need the witness of the community who trusts in God's resurrection power.

The prayers that follow are for the communal expression of that hope. The congregation that articulates its own sorrow, prays together, and proclaims God's goodness can become a healing community for those in the circle of grief.

—∞—

Great Is Your Faithfulness: A Responsive Prayer

My soul is bereft of peace;
    I have forgotten what happiness is; . . .
But this I call to mind,
    and therefore I have hope:
The steadfast love of the LORD never ceases,
    his mercies never come to an end;
they are new every morning;
    great is your faithfulness.
                    (Lamentations 3:17, 21-23)

O God, we have felt the blow of our enemy death. We are bowed down low; gone is all that we had hoped for. Turn our minds toward you and grant us grace to remember your steadfast love.

Great is your faithfulness, O God our Savior.

All that is around us mourns: the roads are empty, the sky is veiled, the flowers fade, the houses sit on lonely ground. Turn our minds toward you and grant us grace to remember your steadfast love.

Great is your faithfulness, O God our Savior.

God, we are living like homeless ones. We are walled in by our grief. Who will comfort us? Who will give us rest? Turn our minds toward you and grant us grace to remember your steadfast love.

Great is your faithfulness, O God our Savior.

We cry out in the night; we pour out our hearts like water before your presence. Hear our cry; take our lifted hands. Turn our minds toward you and grant us grace to remember your steadfast love.

Great is your faithfulness, O God our Savior.

We call on your name, O Lord, from the depths of our sorrow. We long to hear your voice. Turn your face toward us that we may live in the light of your steadfast love.

Great is your faithfulness, O God our Savior.

Take up our cause, O God, and give us reason to live. Scatter the clouds that stop our prayers. Turn your face toward us that we may live in the light of your steadfast love.

Great is your faithfulness, O God our Savior.

Remember, O Lord, what has happened to us. Come near to us that we may hear you when you say, "Do not be afraid." Turn your face toward us that we may live in the light of your steadfast love.

Great is your faithfulness, O God our Savior.

Restore us to yourself, O Lord, that we may be restored. Grant us your tender mercies, new every morning. Our hope is in you, for you have redeemed our life, and you will reign forever. Your steadfast love never ceases.

Great is your faithfulness, O God our Savior. Amen.

We Will Be Like Jesus

See what love the Father has given us, that we should be called children of God; and that is what we are. . . . Beloved, we are God's children now; what we will be has not yet been revealed. What we do know is this: when he is revealed, we will be like him, for we will see him as he is.

(1 John 3:1*a*-2)

God our Creator,
you have made us your children and sent our brother
Jesus Christ to die for us and rise again.
Come near to us with your word of love;
calm our fears and bring us your peace.
Grant us grace to see Jesus as he is
and to know this one thing:
that we and your children who have gone before us
will share in your glory and be like him,
who lives and reigns with you and the Holy Spirit,
now and forever. Amen.

❦

Thanks Be to God for the Victory: A Reading from 1 Corinthians 15

(For two readers)

Now I would remind you, brothers and sisters, of the good news that I proclaimed to you. . . . For I handed on to you as of first importance what I in turn had received: that Christ died for our sins in accordance with the scriptures, and that he was buried, and that he was raised on the third day in accordance with the scriptures, and that he appeared to Cephas, then to the twelve. Then he appeared to more than five hundred brothers and sisters at one time, most of whom are still alive, though some have died. Then he appeared to James, then to all the apostles. Last of all, as to one untimely born, he appeared also to me. . . .

Now if Christ is proclaimed as raised from the dead, how can some of you say there is no resurrection of the dead? If there is no resurrection of the dead, then Christ has not been raised; and if Christ has not been raised, then our proclamation has been in vain and your faith has been in vain. . . .

But in fact Christ has been raised from the dead, the first fruits of those who have died. For since death came through a human being, the resurrection of the dead has also come through a human being; for as all die in Adam, so all will be made alive in Christ. But each in his own order: Christ the first fruits, then at his coming those who belong to Christ. Then comes the end, when he hands over the kingdom to God the Father, after he has destroyed every ruler and every authority and power. For he must reign until he has put all his enemies under his feet. The last enemy to be destroyed is death. For "God has put all things in subjection under his feet." . . .

But someone will ask, "How are the dead raised? With what kind of body do they come?" Fool! What you sow does not come to life unless it dies. . . .

So it is with the resurrection of the dead. What is sown is perishable, what is raised is imperishable. It is sown in dishonor, it is raised in glory. It is sown in weakness, it is raised in power. It is sown a physical body, it is raised a spiritual body. If there is a physical body, there is also a spiritual body. . . .

Listen, I will tell you a mystery! We will not all die, but we will all be changed, in a moment, in the twinkling of an eye, at the last trumpet. For the trumpet will sound, and the dead will be raised imperishable, and we will be changed. For this perishable body must put on imperisha-bility, and this mortal body must put on immortality. When this perishable body puts on imperishability, and this mortal body puts on immortality, then the saying that is written will be fulfilled:
    "Death has been swallowed up in victory."
    "Where, O death, is your victory?
    Where, O death, is your sting?" . . .

Thanks be to God, who gives us the victory through our Lord Jesus Christ.

If Death My Friend and Me Divide

If death my friend and me divide,
thou does not, Lord, my sorrow chide,
or frown my tears to see;
restrained from passionate excess,
thou bidst me mourn in calm distress
for them that rest in thee.

I feel a strong immortal hope,
which bears my mournful spirit up
beneath its mountain load;
redeemed from death, and grief, and pain,
I soon shall find my friend again
within the arms of God.
(Charles Wesley, 1762)

God of compassion,
your Son Jesus blessed those who mourn,
and wept at the grave of his friend Lazarus.
Come near to us with your word of grace,
for we are separated by death from friends who rest in you,
and we carry with us a mountain of grief.
Stay beside us in our distress
and turn us toward the light of hope that pierces the
    clouds.
Help us stand in that light, assured of your promise
to bring us all together in the embrace of your loving
    arms;
through Christ our Lord, who died and lives again. Amen.

Maker of Heaven and Earth

Maker of heaven and earth,
hear me in my need.

**Surround me with your steadfast love,
that I may live again in hope.**

At the surf's edge, I hear the waves' endless roar;
the tide pulls toward the chaos of the sea.

**God of winds and tides,
calm my sea of sadness
that it may not drown your voice of hope.**

The gray clouds gather, lying low on the hills;
my heart, like the sky, is downcast and shuttered.

**God of earth and sky,
open to me the endless glory that your heavens declare.**

I hear the rain against my window,
and I know you are here, even in sorrow.

**God of tender love,
may your mercy fall on me like rain from heaven.**

I find on the path one early flower,
sprung from a seed that fell to earth and died.

**God, you care for the lilies of the field;
hold me that I may hope in you, who raised Jesus to life.**

I lift my eyes to the sky's bright bow of colors,
God's word is as clear as the sun breaking through.

God of promise,
never leave my side; give me your peace.

I am turned by grace to the sunset behind me.
The sky blazes red; gold streaks through the gray.

God of sunsets, you lead us to morning;
take us past clouds to the joy of new day.

❧

The Coming of Our Comforter: A Reading from John 14

(These verses may be read alternately by two groups or by two readers.)

"Do not let your hearts be troubled. Believe in God, believe also in me. In my Father's house there are many dwelling places. If it were not so, would I have told you that I go to prepare a place for you?

"And if I go and prepare a place for you, I will come again and will take you to myself, so that where I am, there you may be also. And you know the way to the place where I am going."

Thomas said to him, "Lord, we do not know where you are going. How can we know the way?"

Jesus said to him, "I am the way, and the truth, and the life. No one comes to the Father except through me. . . .

"I will not leave you orphaned; I am coming to you. In a little while the world will no longer see me, but you will see me; because I live, you also will live. On that day you will know that I am in my Father, and you in me, and I in you.

"They who have my commandments and keep them are those who love me; and those who love me will be loved by my Father, and I will love them and reveal myself to them."

Judas (not Iscariot) said to him, "Lord, how is it that you will reveal yourself to us, and not to the world?"

Jesus answered him, "Those who love me will keep my word, and my Father will love them, and we will come to them and make our home with them. . . .

"But the Advocate, the Holy Spirit, whom the Father will send in my name, will teach you everything, and remind you of all that I have said to you.

"Peace I leave with you; my peace I give to you. I do not give to you as the world gives. Do not let your hearts be troubled, and do not let them be afraid."

Breaking Bread with the Risen Christ

When he was at the table with them, he took bread, blessed and broke it, and gave it to them. Then their eyes were opened, and they recognized him; and he vanished from their sight. They said to each other, "Were not our hearts burning within us while he was talking to us on the road, while he was opening the scriptures to us?" That same hour they got up and returned to Jerusalem; and they found the eleven and their companions gathered together. They were saying, "The Lord has risen indeed."

(Luke 24:30-34*a*)

Gracious God,
you sent your Son Jesus to be the bread of life.
Lead us to the table you have spread,
that we may taste your mercy.
We are empty now, drained by grief,
and our eyes are clouded by tears.
Give us grace to see our risen Lord
in the breaking of the bread.
Let us know the blessing from his lifted hands
and the peace of those who gather in your name.
Fill us with your presence;
comfort us in the company of all
who eat the bread and drink the cup,
in remembrance of your Son Jesus Christ,
now and in the age to come. Amen.

❧

How Lovely Is Your Dwelling Place: A Responsive Prayer Adapted from Psalm 84 and John 14:1-6

Merciful God, we come to you in sorrow, longing for the shelter of your everlasting home. Give us peace.

How lovely is your dwelling place, O Lord of hosts.

Though we are joined in grief, our hearts will sing to you, O living God, for you have promised all things good to those who walk with you. Give us peace.

How lovely is your dwelling place, O Lord of hosts.

Our strength is in you, for in the desert of our sadness, we find your springs of living water, pools from the early rains. Give us peace.

How lovely is your dwelling place, O Lord of hosts.

We know that those who trust in you are blessed, and yet doubt overtakes us before death's dreadful power. Give us hope.

O Lord God of hosts, hear our prayer.

We know that you are our sun and shield, and yet we are overcome by clouds of grief; we feel forsaken and defenseless. Give us hope.

O Lord God of hosts, hear our prayer.

We know that those who leave our sight will never leave

your care; and yet, we are overwhelmed by loneliness and longing for them. Give us hope.

O LORD God of hosts, hear our prayer.

God, in your mercy you grant us your favor. Give us grace to see the light of your face shining on us.

Happy are those who live in your house, ever singing your praise.

God, in your mercy you have made a home for us where even the sparrow finds rest and the swallow a nesting place. Give us grace to be at home with you now.

Happy are those who live in your house, ever singing your praise.

God, in your mercy you sent your Son Jesus Christ, who died and rose to live and return to you. Give us grace to look for his coming again that we may be with him in the place he has prepared.

Happy are those who live in your house, ever singing your praise. Amen.

Greeted by Saints and Angels

In paradisum deducant te Angeli:
in tuo adventu suscipiant te Martyres,
et perducant te in civitatem sanctam, Jerusalem.
Chorus Angelorum te suscipiat,
et cum Lazaro quondam paupere aeternam habeas requiem.

May the angels lead you into paradise;
At your coming may the martyrs receive you,
and lead you to the holy city, Jerusalem.
May the choir of angels greet you,
and may you have eternal rest
with Lazarus, who once was poor. *

God of earth and heaven,
you charge your angels with our care
and bid them keep us safe for our eternal home.
Console us in our grief;
grant that clouds of saints and flights of angels
come to greet our loved ones who have died.
Show us your holy city,
where poor Lazarus is filled with good things,
where mourning, crying, and pain shall be no more.
Give us the peace that casts out fear
and lead us to your new creation in Jesus Christ,
who reigns with you and the Holy Spirit,
now and forever. Amen.

---

* Ancient antiphon used in Christian funeral processions, ca. 800 C.E.;
trans. Fr. Hilary Hayden, O.S.B. Used by permission.

God's Home Is with Mortals: A Reading Adapted from Revelation 21

(For two readers)

Then I saw a new heaven and a new earth; for the first heaven and the first earth had passed away, and the sea was no more.

And I saw the holy city, the new Jerusalem, coming down out of heaven from God, prepared as a bride adorned for her husband. And I heard a loud voice from the throne saying,

"See, the home of God is among mortals.
God will dwell with them;
they will be God's peoples,
and God will be with them
and will wipe every tear from their eyes.
Death will be no more;
mourning and crying and pain will be no more,
for the first things have passed away."

And the one who was seated on the throne said, "See, I am making all things new. Write this, for these words are trustworthy and true."

"It is done! I am the Alpha and the Omega, the beginning and the end. To the thirsty I will give water as a gift from the spring of the water of life. Those who conquer will inherit these things, and I will be their God and they will be my children."

Death Shall Be No More

Death, be not proud, though some have called thee
Mighty and dreadful, for thou art not so;
For those whom thou think'st thou dost overthrow
Die not, poor death, nor yet canst thou kill me.
. . . .
One short sleep past, we wake eternally,
And death shall be no more; death, thou shalt die.

(John Donne, 1609)

God, ruler over all,
you have promised to wipe away every tear,
to put our enemy death under your footstool.
Give us courage now to challenge death's proud hold:
to bless those who mourn,
to watch with the dying,
to stand with those whose lives are little valued,
to hear your wounded creation groan,
to meet all threats that divide one from another,
to defy those whose greed harms your little ones.
Give us grace to fill our lives with hope
and to unfold your gifts of life and love.
In the name of your Son, to whom you gave the victory.
  Amen.

Nothing Separates Us from Christ's Love: A Reading Adapted from Romans 8

(For two readers)

There is therefore now no condemnation for those who are in Christ Jesus. For the law of the Spirit of life in Christ Jesus has set you free from the law of sin and of death.

If the Spirit of the One who raised Jesus from the dead dwells in you, the One who raised Christ from the dead will give life to your mortal bodies also through God's Spirit that dwells in you.

For all who are led by the Spirit of God are children of God. For you did not receive a spirit of slavery to fall back into fear, but you have received a spirit of adoption. When we cry, "Abba! Father!" it is that very Spirit bearing witness with our spirit that we are children of God, and if children, then heirs, heirs of God and joint heirs with Christ—if, in fact, we suffer with him so that we may also be glorified with him.

I consider that the sufferings of this present time are not worth comparing with the glory about to be revealed to us. For the creation waits with eager longing for the revealing of the children of God; for the creation was subjected to futility, not of its own will but by the will

of the one who subjected it, in hope that the creation itself will be set free from its bondage to decay and will obtain the freedom of the glory of the children of God.

We know that the whole creation has been groaning in labor pains until now; and not only the creation, but we ourselves, who have the first fruits of the Spirit, groan inwardly while we wait for adoption, the redemption of our bodies.

For in hope we were saved. Now hope that is seen is not hope. For who hopes for what is seen? But if we hope for what we do not see, we wait for it with patience.

Likewise the Spirit helps us in our weakness; for we do not know how to pray as we ought, but that very Spirit intercedes with sighs too deep for words. And God, who searches the heart, knows what is the mind of the Spirit, because the Spirit intercedes for the saints according to the will of God.

We know that all things work together for good for those who love God, who are called according to his purpose.

What then are we to say about these things? If God is for us, who is against us? God who did not withhold his own Son, but gave him up for all of us, will God not with him also give us everything else? Who will bring any charge against God's elect? It is God who justifies. Who is to condemn?

It is Christ Jesus, who died, yes, who was raised, who is at the right hand of God, who indeed intercedes for us. Who will separate us from the love of Christ? Will hardship, or distress, or persecution, or famine, or nakedness, or peril, or sword?

For I am convinced that neither death, nor life, nor angels, nor rulers, nor things present, nor things to come, nor powers, nor height, nor depth, nor anything else in all creation, will be able to separate us from the love of God in Christ Jesus our Lord. No, in all these things we are more than conquerors through him who loved us. Let us hold on to Jesus' love that knows no bounds.

A Litany for Those in the Circle of Grief

O God, Creator and Father, from whom every family on earth and heaven is named,
Have mercy on us.
O Son of God, Jesus Christ, whose life freely given redeems the world,
Have mercy on us.
O Holy Spirit of God, who blesses the faithful and gives us peace,
Have mercy on us.
O Lord our God, holy, blessed, and glorious Trinity,
Have mercy on us.

God of mercy, you have promised to wipe out all our sins and remember no more the sins of our ancestors: Save us by your mercy and heal us.
From pride, deceit, and prejudice; from envy and false affection,
Merciful God, deliver us.
From all oppression, violence, and injustice,
Merciful God, deliver us.
From all evil and at last from death itself,
Merciful God, deliver us.

God of grace, your Son Jesus left his place in glory, was born to Mary, and submitted to our human weakness, even death, for the sake of the world. By his birth and life, by his death and glorious resurrection, by his ascension and the coming of the Holy Spirit,
Merciful God, deliver us.

Grant, O Lord, that wars may cease and all nations may live in freedom and peace.
Lord, in your mercy,
hear our prayer.

Grant, good Lord, that no one may be held unjustly, that we remember to visit the prisoners, and that those who hold captives may look toward them with kindness.
Lord, in your mercy,
hear our prayer.

Grant, O Lord, protection for those in danger: those who travel, those who put their lives at risk for others, and those who engage in perilous work; Lord, in your mercy,
hear our prayer.

Grant, good Lord, provision and strength for all women in childbirth and protection for all children, especially the homeless and those whose homes are torn by conflict.
Lord, in your mercy,
hear our prayer.

Grant, O Lord, that we may bring the goodness of your presence to the lonely and to those who suffer in mind, body, and spirit.
Lord, in your mercy,
hear our prayer.

Grant, good Lord, that we may give assurance to those in doubt, confidence to those with troubled minds, and faithfulness to those who fail to see your grace.
Lord, in your mercy,
hear our prayer.

Grant, O Lord, that those who grieve may know your blessing, receive your mercies, which are new every morning, and find in you their comfort and their hope.
Lord, in your mercy,
hear our prayer.

Grant, good Lord, that those who have died find in you eternal life and peace. Give to all the faithful, especially to *[Name]*, whose death we mourn, rest in the home you have prepared. Reunite us at last in the company of saints who live in Christ's glorious reign.
Lord, in your mercy,
hear our prayer.

Lamb of God, you take away the sin of the world;
have mercy on us.
Lamb of God, you take away the sin of the world;
have mercy on us.
Lamb of God, you take away the sin of the world;
grant us peace.

Lord, have mercy on us.
Christ, have mercy on us.
Lord, have mercy on us.

(The Lord's Prayer may be said.)

Gracious God, you promised through your beloved Son that when we are gathered in his name you will be with us and hear our prayers. Grant us now, O Lord, our desires and petitions, that we may live in your favor. Give us even now the knowledge of your truth and, in the age to come, life and joy with all the company of heaven. Graciously hear us in the name of Jesus, our Savior, who reigns with you and the Holy Spirit, one God, now and forever. **Amen.**

The grace of our Lord Jesus Christ, and the love of God, and the communion of the Holy Spirit, be with us all, now and evermore. **Amen.**

Psalm 90: Three Prayers

Turn, O Lord! How long?
Have compassion on your servants!
Satisfy us in the morning with your steadfast love,
so that we may rejoice and be glad all our days.
(Psalm 90:13-14)

God of compassion,
we trust to you our loved ones,
now in your sight though not in ours.
Our sadness never leaves us, and we are tired;
we are worn out with longing for the dawn.
Heal us from the weariness of grief;
refresh us and lift our eyes to your light.
Give us grace to know again the joy of friends,
the warm embrace of those around us,
the health of waking from hope-filled dreams.
Keep safe our memory of those parted from us by death,
and teach us to live in hope as they would have us do.
Send us into the new day you open before us
with the strength to be glad in the work you give us.
Let the splendor of your face shine on us
and give us peace.
In the name of Jesus, who is our peace. Amen.

Before the hills in order stood,
or earth received her frame,
from everlasting, thou art God,
to endless years the same.

A thousand ages, in thy sight,
are like an evening gone;
short as the watch that ends the night,
before the rising sun.

O God, our help in ages past,
our hope for years to come;
be thou our guide while life shall last,
and our eternal home.
(Isaac Watts, 1719)

O God, our help and hope,
you have been our home
from generation to generation.
Guard us in life and shelter us.
We ask that we and those we love
enjoy good health our seventy or eighty years,
that we might live together in your favor.
Make our days glad
and bless the work we do.
Lead us through the evening watch
and to the rising sun.
For though you return us to dust
and sweep away the years,
we ask your grace to hope
that past sorrows will give way to new joy,
that a thousand years singing your praise
will pass like a single day
when we have joined the glorious dance
in your unbroken circle of love.
In the name of Jesus your Son. Amen.

Our years come to an end like a sigh.
The days of our life are seventy years,
or perhaps eighty, if we are strong;
even then their span is only toil and trouble;
they are soon gone, and we fly away.
(Psalm 90:9b-10)

Some glad morning when this life is o'er, I'll fly away.
To a home on God's celestial shore, I'll fly away.
(Albert E. Brumley)

71

God of our deepest longing,
your glory filled the earth before the mountains rose:
Hold us through the trouble of our days.
Hear our sighs; strengthen us in the face of death.
Heal us with the gladness of your love in the morning.
Give us your hand and lift us with the warm breath of
    your Spirit,
and we will fly away to you, our home, now and forever.
In the name of Jesus,
who rose from death and lives with you. Amen.

❧

A House Not Made with Hands

For we know that if the earthly tent we live in is
destroyed, we have a building from God, a house not
made with hands, eternal in the heavens. For in this tent
we groan, longing to be clothed with our heavenly
dwelling . . . because we wish not to be unclothed but to
be further clothed, so that what is mortal may be
swallowed up by life. He who has prepared us for this very
thing is God, who has given us the Spirit as a guarantee.
(2 Corinthians 5:1-2, 4*b*-5)

O God, builder and comforter,
you have prepared for us a house of your own making,
a home eternal in the heavens
with the Spirit's guarantee.
Hear our cry; free us from death's stifling tent,
from the anguish of losing those we love.
Strengthen our faith;
stay with us through our doubt and distress.
Give us voices to sing your praise,
for we long to be clothed once more by you
and swallowed up by life.
In the name of Jesus, the way, the truth, the life. Amen.

〜✆

The Risen Christ Appears to Mary Magdalene: A Reading from John 20:1-18

(For two readers)

Early on the first day of the week, while it was still dark, Mary Magdalene came to the tomb and saw that the stone had been removed from the tomb. So she ran and went to Simon Peter and the other disciple, the one whom Jesus loved, and said to them, "They have taken the Lord out of the tomb, and we do not know where they have laid him."

Then Peter and the other disciple set out and went toward the tomb. The two were running together, but the other disciple outran Peter and reached the tomb first. He bent down to look in and saw the linen wrappings lying there, but he did not go in.

Then Simon Peter came, following him, and went into the tomb. He saw the linen wrappings lying there, and the cloth that had been on Jesus' head, not lying with the linen wrappings but rolled up in a place by itself. Then the other disciple, who reached the tomb first, also went in, and he saw and believed; for as yet they did not understand the scripture, that he must rise from the dead. Then the disciples returned to their homes.

But Mary stood weeping outside the tomb. As she wept, she bent over to look into the tomb; and she saw two angels in white, sitting where the body of Jesus had been lying, one at the head and the other at the feet.

They said to her, "Woman, why are you weeping?"

She said to them, "They have taken away my Lord, and I do not know where they have laid him."

When she had said this, she turned around and saw Jesus standing there, but she did not know that it was Jesus. Jesus said to her, "Woman, why are you weeping? Whom are you looking for?"

Supposing him to be the gardener, she said to him, "Sir, if you have carried him away, tell me where you have laid him, and I will take him away."

Jesus said to her, "Mary!" She turned and said to him in Hebrew, "Rabbouni!" (which means Teacher).

Jesus said to her, "Do not hold on to me, because I have not yet ascended to the Father. But go to my brothers and say to them, 'I am ascending to my Father and your Father, to my God and your God.' "

Mary Magdalene went and announced to the disciples, "I have seen the Lord"; and she told them that he had said these things to her.

God Will Raise Us Also with Jesus: A Responsive Prayer

The one who raised the Lord Jesus will raise us also with Jesus, and will bring us with you into his presence. Yes, everything is for your sake, so that grace, as it extends to more and more people, may increase thanksgiving, to the glory of God.

(2 Corinthians 4:14-15)

God of life, you raised Jesus from the dead;
have mercy on us and on those who have died.

Bring us, O God, into your presence.

God of hope, you will raise us also with Jesus;
have mercy on us and take away our fear.

Bring us, O God, into your presence.

God of grace, you offer life to the whole world;
have mercy on us and lead us to open wide our arms.

Bring us, O God, into your presence.

God of peace, you give us your glory and welcome us
home; have mercy on us and increase our songs of praise.

**Bring us into your presence with songs of thanksgiving.
In Jesus' name. Amen.**

V

A Liturgy for the Burying or Scattering of Ashes

If the ashes of the deceased are buried or scattered after a period of time has elapsed since the death, or if there is no other memorial service this service may be used. A liturgy that recalls the words of hope and thanksgiving proclaimed in services of remembrance for someone who has died is appropriate. If the ashes are to be placed in a columbarium located within a church, the pascal candle and other symbols of baptism may be used. For outdoor services, an arrangement that includes sheaves of wheat, grapes, and a bowl of water may be placed on a table with the urn.

—ഡ—

The Gathering

Leader:
"I am the resurrection and the life," says the Lord. "Those who believe in me, even though they die, will live, and everyone one who lives and believes in me will never die" (John 11:25-26).

We gather in the name of Jesus Christ to give thanks for the life of *[Name]* and to remember that *[he/she]* is a child of God, baptized at the fount of life and nourished at God's table. May we praise God and give God thanks for Jesus Christ, who by his death and resurrection, has led the way to life. Alleluia!

(Hymn; suggestions: "Joyful, Joyful, We Adore Thee," "For the Beauty of the Earth")

The Word of God

Leader:
Let us listen to God's word and spend a few moments in silent reflection.

Psalm 103:11-18 (adapted)

(Read antiphonally by two voices or two groups)

For as the heavens are high above the earth,
   so great is the Lord's steadfast love toward the faithful;

as far as the east is from the west,
   so far does the LORD remove our transgressions from us.

As a father has compassion for his children,
so the LORD has compassion for those who fear him.

For the LORD knows how we were made;
and remembers that we are dust.

As for mortals, their days are like grass;
they flourish like a flower of the field;
for the wind passes over it, and it is gone,
and its place knows it no more.

But the steadfast love of the LORD is from everlasting to
everlasting
upon the faithful,
and righteousness of the LORD to children's children.

(Silence is kept.)

John 12:20-26*a*

Reader:
Now among those who went up to worship at the festival
were some Greeks. They came to Philip, who was from
Bethsaida in Galilee, and said to him, "Sir, we wish to see
Jesus." Philip went and told Andrew; then Andrew and
Philip went and told Jesus. Jesus answered them, "The
hour has come for the Son of Man to be glorified. Very
truly, I tell you, unless a grain of wheat falls into the earth
and dies, it remains just a single grain; but if it dies, it
bears much fruit. Those who love their life lose it, and
those who hate their life in this world will keep it for eternal life. Whoever serves me must follow me, and where I
am, there will my servant be also.

(Silence is kept.)

1 John 3:1-2

Reader:
See what love the Father has given us, that we should be called children of God; and that is what we are. . . .
Beloved, we are God's children now; what we will be has not yet been revealed. What we do know is this: when he is revealed, we will be like him, for we will see him as he is.

(Silence is kept.)

The Acts of Faith

Leader:
Let us pray.

God of life, you gave us birth,
and you hold us even in death.
Accept now our prayers of thanksgiving for the life of
    [Name].
Comfort us with the assurance that *[she/he]* is at rest with
    you.
Open our eyes to the beauty of your creation,
where all that lives returns to the earth
and never leaves your care.
Grant us grace to live in your circle of hope,
where we are surrounded by your love
and move in company with our risen Lord.
Give us courage to commit our *[brother/sister Name]* to
    your keeping,
in steadfast hope of the coming day of resurrection.
Through Jesus our Savior. Amen.

Our Father, who art in heaven,
hallowed be thy name.
Thy kingdom come,
thy will be done on earth as it is in heaven.
Give us this day our daily bread.
And forgive us our trespasses,
as we forgive those who trespass against us.
And lead us not into temptation,
but deliver us from evil.
For thine is the kingdom, and the power, and the glory,
forever. Amen.

*(The urn is placed in the ground or columbarium. If the ashes
are to be scattered, the dispersal should be done with care, hold-
ing the urn low to the ground, and regarding the direction of
the wind.)*

Leader:
In sure and certain hope of the resurrection to eternal life
through our Lord Jesus Christ,
we commend to our gracious God our *[brother/sister
Name]*,
and we commit *[his/her]* ashes to be returned to the
elements;
ashes to ashes, dust to dust.
May God in faithful mercy
bring us all, the living and departed,
to a joyful resurrection in the fullness of God's time.
In Jesus' name. Amen.

*(If the ashes are buried on family land, the family and friends
may wish to plant a tree in memory of the deceased. Revelation
22:1-7 may be read before the tree is placed and watered. If
planting is not possible, each participant may bring one flower
to place appropriately near the ashes as a hymn is sung.)*

(Hymn; suggestions: "Now Thank We All Our God," "Steal Away to Jesus")

Going Forth

The Peace

Leader: The peace of the Lord be with you always.
People: **And also with you.**
Leader: Let us now exchange greetings of encouragement and peace.

Dismissal with Blessing

Let us go from this place renewed in Spirit,
ready to bear God's love to others
and tell with the witness of our lives the story of God's
only Son, who was sent to die for us
and be raised from the dead so that
all the world might have abundant life.

May the God of hope
fill you with all joy and peace in believing,
so that you may abound in hope
by the power of the Holy Spirit. Amen.

VI

A Service of Remembrance for the Anniversary of a Death

The participants gather around a table that holds a cross or an open Bible, a lighted candle, and a picture of the deceased or other objects associated with him/her. Each family or participant is asked ahead of time to bring a candle (one that can stand on its own) to place on the table during the ritual.

—⁂—

The Gathering

Leader:
A year ago we were parted by death from our friend
[Name], whose memory fills our nights and days. The pain
of loss has softer edges now, but the sadness of *[his/her]*
absence stays, even as we know the comfort of God's
presence. We recall that Jesus wept with Mary and Martha
at the grave of Lazarus and looks with compassion on all
who grieve. We are here to remember *[Name]* and give
thanks for *[his/her]* life. Together we hear Jesus' tender
voice calling: "Come to me, all you that are weary and are
carrying heavy burdens, and I will give you rest!"
(Matthew 11:28).

*(Hymn; suggestions: "Shall We Gather at the River," "Come,
Ye Disconsolate," "For All the Saints")*

The Word of God

An Adapted Reading from Psalm 145:8-18, 21

*(The verses are read alternately by men and women or by two
readers.)*

The LORD is gracious and merciful,
   slow to anger and abounding in steadfast love.

**O LORD, you are good to all,
   your compassion is over all that you have made.**

All your works shall give thanks to you, O LORD,
   and all your faithful shall bless you.

**They shall speak of the glory of your kingdom,
   and tell of your power,**

to make known to all people your mighty deeds,
and the glorious splendor of your kingdom.

**Your kingdom is an everlasting kingdom,
and your dominion endures throughout all
generations.**

O LORD, you are faithful in all your words,
and gracious in all your deeds.

**The LORD upholds all who are falling,
and raises up all who are bowed down.**

The eyes of all look to you,
and you give them their food in due season.

**You open your hand,
satisfying the desire of every living thing.**

O LORD, you are just in all your ways,
and kind in all your doings.
You are near to all who call on you,
to all who call on you in truth.

**My mouth will speak the praise of the LORD,
and all flesh will bless God's holy name forever and
ever.**

*(Music. A solo instrument or a recording may be played.
Suggestions: "Laudate Dominum" from Mozart's* Vesperae
solemnes de Confessore *[K 139]; Bach's "Sheep May Safely
Graze"; Dorsey's "Precious Lord, Take My Hand"; or a favorite
selection of the deceased.)*

The Coming of the Light:
Selected New Testament Readings

(These verses may be read by two or more readers.)

In the beginning was the Word, and the Word was with God, and the Word was God. He was in the beginning with God. All things came into being through him, and without him not one thing came into being. What has come into being in him was life, and the life was the light of all people. The light shines in the darkness, and the darkness did not overcome it. (John 1:1-5)

Again Jesus spoke to them, saying, "I am the light of the world. Whoever follows me will never walk in darkness but will have the light of life." (John 8:12)

"You are the light of the world. A city built on a hill cannot be hid. No one after lighting a lamp puts it under the bushel basket, but on the lampstand, and it gives light to all in the house. In the same way, let your light shine before others, so that they may see your good works and give glory to your Father in heaven." (Matthew 5:14-16)

May you be made strong with all the strength that comes from [God's] glorious power, and may you be prepared to endure everything with patience, while joyfully giving thanks to the Father, who has enabled you to share in the inheritance of the saints in the light. [God] has rescued us from the power of darkness and transferred us into the kingdom of his beloved Son, in whom we have redemption, the forgiveness of sins. He is the image of the invisible God, the firstborn of all creation; for in him all things in heaven and on earth were created, things visible and invisible, whether thrones or dominions or rulers or powers—all things have been created through him and for him. He himself is before all things, and in him all things hold together. He is the head of the body, the church; he is the beginning, the firstborn from the dead, so that he might come to have first place in everything. For in him all the fullness of God was pleased to dwell. (Colossians 1:11-19)

Acts of Remembrance

Readings and Stories

(Participants have been asked to prepare a story about the person or a brief reading.)

Lighting of the Candles

Leader:
We have brought candles to light in *[Name's]* memory and to remind us that the light of God's grace still shines through those who blessed us in their lives. We light these candles in thanksgiving for God's promise that we will be together again in God's new creation, where no light is needed but the light of God's wonderful face.

   As we bring our candles forward let us join in singing "Blest Be the Tie That Binds."

(Other suggestions: "We Are Marching in the Light of God," "When the Saints Go Marching In")

(During the singing, each participant in turn brings a candle to the table, lights it from the center candle, and places it on the table.)

Leader:
Let us each give a prayer of thanksgiving for *[Name]*. Please close your prayer by saying: **"Thank you, God, for [Name]. We are blessed by [his/her] memory. Amen."**

87

Closing Prayer

Leader:
Gracious God, we thank you for the life of *[Name]* and for the joy of loving and being loved by *[him/her]*. We praise you for the great company of your saints who, though they have died, are present with us in worship and service. We await with them Christ's coming in glory. Through Jesus Christ, who lived and died and lives again to reign with you and the Holy Spirit. **Amen.**

(Hymn; suggestions: "There Is a Balm in Gilead," "O God, Our Help in Ages Past," "My Lord, What a Morning")

VII

Grief and Prayer Through the Church Year

In our culture there is a growing tendency, even in the popular media, to cry out for a moment of closure after events that involve the loss of human life. We often hear the plea for a ceremony of remembrance that will help the families of airplane crashes, violent crimes, and natural disasters. This public memorializing is worthwhile, but no one act or ritual can stop the grief and put matters completely to rest. And when an individual dies in ordinary circumstances, there may be little public acknowledgment, little chance for the family to grieve with others. The time of mourning after the death of a close loved one is often not easily brought to an end; sadness may linger even when life goes on and the bereaved have learned to cope. A Christian funeral, with its marvelous affirmation of God's power for life, is the beginning, not the end, of the healing that must take place. As pastors and friends, we know that the embrace of the sorrowing by a praying community is a continuing agent of comfort and hope, and we are in it for the long haul.

The habit of praying in tune with the church year calendar is a long-standing way of marking time that has implications for a period of mourning. The liturgical seasons correspond to our faith stories of death and resurrection and the promised triumph of God's gift of life. The rhythms of grief and hope experienced after a loss parallel the Christmas and Easter cycles with their weeks of somber waiting followed by celebrations of new life. Each observance in the church calendar offers a passage that leads to the door of hope and brings us into the compass of resurrection.

The prayers in this section can be used to give liturgical

context at funerals and at various occasions throughout the year. They offer suggestions for including the grieving in our continuing life of common prayer. The need to pray at special times, such as Christmas and Easter, for those in the community who have lost loved ones during the year is understood, but other observances have special significance for grief and healing as well. The less frequently observed commemorations on the calendar can serve as reminders to pray for the sorrowing at various church events, through prayers in groups or households, or on pastoral visits. Petitions for those who have died and those who mourn are traditionally included in the Prayers of the People every Sunday, and these petitions can make the connection to the liturgical seasons as well.

Now a word about the saints: the observance of saints' days is not usual in the Reformation tradition because we understand ourselves as a community of believers where no one of us is given a place higher than the other. We are all called by God and set apart to be saints; God has already blessed us. That does not mean we have no reason to commemorate saints. The communion of saints is deeply woven into our understanding of the resurrected life; it recurs in our creeds, and we sing with great joy: "For all the saints, who from their labors rest." We do not pray to the saints, but we pray with the saints, for we are emboldened by that great "cloud of witnesses" (Hebrews 12:1).

I have therefore included three representative saints' days in the prayer calendar that follows. These three can speak for the hosts of saints who are standing ready to welcome us home. We can at times choose to pray with a specific saint, one known to us through tradition or Scripture, or a person we have known in life. The biblical saints in particular can help us focus our prayers on the promises we call on God to remember, and can give us assurance that God will hear our prayer. The biblical saints have particular resonance with the grieving and show God's blessing on those who mourn. They also signify the resurrection.

The three saints I have chosen for these prayers all have strong associations with the experience of death and dying, and they illuminate by their lives our understanding of God's never-ending care for us. Sometimes we long to pray but the words will not come, and we need just such an association. Sometimes choosing a saint to pray with, by the chance that the saint's day falls near the anniversary of a death or on the deceased person's birthday, may bring unexpected grace.

In choosing scripture and prayers for a funeral or memorial service, moreover, we may want to consider the liturgical season. Often the lectionary readings for a particular church year observance that falls near the day of the funeral will open our eyes to God's promise of eternal life in new ways. Being led by the Scriptures associated with a season or celebration is one avenue to preaching and living the gospel of Jesus Christ at the time of a death. The liturgical calendar offers an open invitation, at the funeral and through the year, to connect those standing in the circle of grief with the central story of our faith, the story of our God who lives among us and brings life out of death.

—w—

❧

A Prayer Calendar for Those Standing in the Circle of Grief

Advent

Isaiah 61:1-4, 8-12; Psalm 80:1-7, 17-19; Revelation 22:12-17, 20-21; Luke 1:26-38

During the Advent season we express our longing in hymns, scripture, and prayer for the coming again of Jesus Christ in glory. We recognize the forces of death at work around us and seek to prepare for the time when God's reign will come in its fullness. A part of this longing is the desire to be reunited with loved ones in the home that God has prepared for us. These are themes that speak to those who have experienced loss and are especially sad during the days leading to Christmas. During Advent, some congregations offer special services for families and individuals for whom a recent loss will be sharply felt at Christmas.

> O, come, thou Dayspring, come and cheer
> our spirits by thine advent here;
> disperse the gloomy clouds of night,
> and death's dark shadows put to flight.
> (9th-century Latin hymn)

True man, yet very God, from sin and death now save us, and share our every load.
("Lo, How a Rose E'er Blooming," *The Hymnal*, 1940)

Come, long-expected Jesus,
hope of all the earth,
joy of longing hearts.
Release us from our fears and give us rest.
Stay with us through days of doubt and discord
that we may know your peace.
Keep those we love in life and death in your embrace.
Return to bring your glorious reign in all the world,
for you are all compassion; pure, unbounded love,
and we wait for your new creation
when we will join the song of praise to the risen One,
in whose name we pray. Amen.

Christmas

Isaiah 52:7-10; Psalm 98; Hebrews 1:1-4 (5-12); John 1:1-14

The child Mary bore and wrapped in swaddling clothes,
as his body was later wrapped in grave clothes to be left
behind in the empty tomb, was born to die and be raised
from death. Jesus' birth brought, as Isaiah prophesied, the
light of God's glory upon us, dispersing the gloom that cov-
ers the earth and all its peoples. This child, at home with
seekers and mourners, would be the one through whom
God finds a home with mortals so that, finally, God can
wipe every tear from every eye: "Death will be no more;
mourning and crying and pain will be no more, for the first
things have passed away" (Revelation 21.4). Thus Christmas is always celebrated as a feast of the resurrection.

> Good Christian friends, rejoice with heart and soul and
> voice;
> now ye need not fear the grave; News, news!
> Jesus Christ was born to save!
> (14th-century Latin hymn)

Light and life to all he brings; risen with healing in his
  wings.
Mild he lays his glory by, born that we no more may die,
born to raise us from the earth, born to give us second birth.
Hark! the herald angels sing, "Glory to the newborn King!"
("Hark! The Herald Angels Sing," Charles Wesley, 1739)

God of glory,
your angels sang a new song on the mountains;
they told good news to the shepherds.
Grant that those in sorrow this day
may look to the singing hills,
hear the sea roar, the floods clap,
and know the peace of your presence.
We thank you for the victory that is yours, O God,
for the gift of your Son, who laid down his glory
and was born in a stable cave
that he might one day die for us
and rise to leave an empty cave behind.
We thank you for the life that Christ's coming brings.
Grant us grace to know him as one of us,
who shared our weakness and died our death
that we may one day live with him.
We ask that even now we know your life-giving love
and walk in newness of life all our days.
Through Jesus Christ, holy Child and Savior. Amen.

Saint Stephen (December 26)

*Jeremiah 26:1-9, 12-15; Psalm 31; Acts 6:8–7:2a, 51c-60;
Matthew 23:34-39*

Why did the shapers of the liturgical calendar see fit to
place the sad commemoration of a martyr's death on the
day after Christmas? Mourning, our culture tells us, is out
of place at Christmas; yet it is a crucial part of the story.
Christmas is a time of remembering—and rejoicing—that

the Word became flesh, obedient unto death, so that we might have life. Prayers on Saint Stephen's Day may help families mark the death of someone they love, especially if that person died at Christmas. Stephen's story reminds us of his concern for the poor, and, most significantly, Stephen, sure of being received by Christ at the right hand of God, teaches us how to die. We see through the memory of his death, at a time when we rejoice in the new life Jesus brings, that birth and death are never far from each other and that the center of our Christmas celebration is the remembrance of Jesus' birth, life, death, and resurrection.

> Good King Wenceslas looked out on the Feast of
>   Stephen,
> when the snow lay round about, deep and crisp, and
>   even:
> Brightly shone the moon that night, though the frost
>   was cruel,
> when a poor man came in sight, gathering winter fuel.
> . . . .
> "Bring me flesh, and bring me wine, bring me pine-logs
>   hither:
> Thou and I will see him dine, when we bear them
>   thither."
> Page and monarch, forth they went, forth they went
>   together;
> through the rude wind's wild lament and the bitter
>   weather.
> . . . .
> Therefore, Christian [souls], be sure, wealth or rank
>   possessing,
> ye who now will bless the poor shall yourselves find
>   blessing.
>
> ("Good King Wenceslas")

Merciful God,
your servant Stephen was full of grace and power,
serving the poor and giving witness to your love.
Grant us his kindness, courage, and faith
that we may meet death with our eyes on the risen Lord.
God, in our lonely grief, we cannot sing of Christmas joy:
Gather us under your wings as a mother hen shelters her
    chicks.
You knew at his birth your Son had come to die;
now share our sorrow,
be our comfort and hope in life and in death,
that we and those we love may one day rise again like
    Jesus,
who reigns with you and the Holy Spirit, now and
    forever. Amen.

Epiphany

Isaiah 60:1-6; Psalm 72:1-7, 10-14; Ephesians 3:1-12; Matthew 2:1-12

The visit of the Magi to the child Jesus is set in a story of political intrigue. Beginning with Herod's plot to kill Jesus and ending with "Rachel weeping for her children" (Matthew 2:18), the story leaves no doubt that death is everywhere. Innocents slaughtered in the midst of a political power play, and mothers unconsoled are the world Jesus came to save. In T. S. Eliot's poem "Journey of the Magi," the Magi are confused by what they find at the end of their journey—a baby marked for death—and they ask if they were led to Bethlehem for a birth or a death; the birth they find in Bethlehem was, they say, "Hard and bitter agony for us, like Death, our death."* Our death and our personal experiences of grief and loss are woven

---

* T. S. Eliot, "Journey of the Magi," *The Complete Poems and Plays, 1909–1950* (New York: Harcourt Brace & World, 1952), 68.

into this story, and we long, even as we celebrate the coming of the light, for God's final victory over the forces of death.

> Myrrh is mine; its bitter perfume breathes a life of
>   gathering gloom;
> sorrowing, sighing, bleeding, dying, sealed in the
>   stone-cold tomb.
> Glorious now behold him arise; King and God and
>   sacrifice:
> Alleluia, Alleluia, sounds through the earth and skies.

> O star of wonder, star of light, star with royal beauty
>   bright,
> westward leading, still proceeding, guide us to thy
>   perfect light.
>   ("We Three Kings," John H. Hopkins, Jr., 1857)

God of star-gazers and wanderers,
you led the Magi to the child at Bethlehem.
Now lead us to the light of Jesus,
born in death's shadow that he might bring life.
Give us courage to leave familiar ground,
and guide our journeys that we may bear your gift of
    love.
Be with those caught in distant landscapes,
the seekers and the mourners, longing for home.
Hear the cry of Rachel weeping,
grieving with mothers everywhere
whose children have no chance at life.
As you showed the Magi Herod's treachery,
open our eyes to systems and tyrants
that use death to serve their own designs.
Make us agents of your life-giving power;
in the name of Jesus, sought by all who love life. Amen.

Presentation of the Lord (February 2)

Malachi 3:1-4; Psalm 84; Hebrews 2:14-18; Luke 3:22-40

The story of Jesus' presentation in the temple reveals through the characters of Anna and Simeon the identity of this baby who came to bless those who mourn. Blessed is Anna who praised God for her Savior, proclaiming his saving grace to all she met. The prophet Anna, who, according to Luke, spent her life in God's house praying and fasting, may well have taken the role of official mourner when the grief-stricken entered the temple; she had mourned her husband for most of her years and knew how to cry with others. Her mourning led to her praising. Blessed is Simeon, who saw the nearness of his own death and lived to see the light God had sent to the world. This is a feast of light, revealing God's promises and bringing hope to those who live in the shadow of death.

> Lord, let your servant
> now die in peace,
> for you kept your promise.
>
> With my own eyes
> I see the salvation
> you prepared for all peoples:
>
> a light of revelation for the Gentiles
> and glory to your people Israel.*
> (Canticle of Simeon)

God, you are the source of all light;
you fulfilled the hope of Simeon and Anna, who did not
die until they welcomed the Messiah.
May we, who have received your gifts beyond measure,

---

* The English translation of the Canticle of Simeon, from *The Liturgical Psalter* © 1995, International Committee on English in the Liturgy, Inc. All rights reserved.

prepare to meet Christ Jesus when he comes to bring us
  home.
May we, who praise your glory,
walk in the path of your love
and come to the light that shines forever.
Give us peace; free us from our fear of death,
for we have seen the One whose love
will destroy the power of death. In the name of the risen
Christ. Amen.

Lent

*Isaiah 43:16-21; Psalm 126; 2 Corinthians 5:17–6:2; John
3:1-17*

At the beginning of Lent we pray that the ashes may be
a sign of our mortality, reminding us that only by God's
gracious gift are we given everlasting life through Christ
Jesus our Savior. We are told to remember that we are
dust and will return to dust. Those facing terminal illness
and those who have recently lost loved ones need no such
reminder and, in fact, are able to witness to death's reality
among us. But at this season we are also asked to remember our baptism and be thankful. Thus we join with the
grieving in a discipline of life lived united through baptism with Christ. In our baptism, according to Paul, we
share with Christ a death like his and wait on the promise
of being "united with him in a resurrection like his"
(Romans 6:5). Accepting our mortality never means living
without hope of life.

> What wondrous love is this, O my soul, O my soul,
> What wondrous love is this, O my soul!
> What wondrous love is this that caused the Lord of life
> to lay aside his crown for my soul, for my soul,
> to lay aside his crown for my soul.

And when from death I'm free, I'll sing on, I'll sing on,
And when from death I'm free, I'll sing on;
And when from death I'm free, I'll sing and joyful be,
and through eternity I'll sing on, I'll sing on,
and through eternity, I'll sing on. (USA folk hymn)

God, our deliverer,
You created us from the dust of the earth
and breathed your life into us.
Guide our thoughts; show us your marvelous ways;
for though we were slaves to death, you gave us freedom.
Comfort those who now face death and those who mourn.
Grant us grace to feel again your breath of life;
for though we return to dust,
you have promised us a new creation in Jesus Christ,
who set his face toward the cross
that we might walk with him toward life.
In his name we pray. Amen.

Palm Sunday

*Isaiah 50:4-9a; Psalm 118:1-2, 19-29; Philippians 2:5-11;
Matthew 21:1-11*

On Palm Sunday, we celebrate Jesus' riding toward
Jerusalem as the people shout "Hosanna! God save us!"
Underneath the festivity, there is a subtext of danger and
despair: Jesus knows he is riding to his own death, and
the people know their desperate need for salvation. Jesus
is hailed as the King of Peace by his followers who have
read the Hebrew Prophets, and yet his presence signals
conflict. His title is officially bestowed by the judge who
sentences him to die, and it is through his lifting up on
the cross that he reigns exalted. Jesus became in every
way like us and, by his acceptance of death, put an end to
death's power to enslave us. For this he has been highly
exalted and given a name that is above every name. We

live in a Palm Sunday world; the full joy of Easter is not
yet with us, and there is weeping in the days to come. But
we know that we are headed to Easter and that Jesus,
who knows firsthand the pain of death, is with us.

> King Jesus rides on a milk-white horse,
>   No man can a-hinder me;
> The river of Jordan he did cross,
>   no man can a-hinder me.
> Ride on, King Jesus,
>   no man can a-hinder me.
>   (African American spiritual)

> He left his Father's throne above
> (so free, so infinite his grace!),
> emptied himself of all but love,
> and bled for Adam's helpless race.
> 'Tis mercy all, immense and free,
> for O my God, it found out me!
> ("And Can It Be That I Should Gain,"
>   Charles Wesley, 1739)

God, our salvation,
your steadfast love endures forever.
Come to us in our anguish;
sustain us with your word of hope.
Open to us the gates of justice
that we might set our face against despair and death.
Morning by morning, wake us with your mercies.
Lift our eyes to the crucified One, Jesus Christ,
who left your side and became obedient to death.
Lift our hearts to the exalted One,
who knows our fears and sorrows
and will lift us all to you.
We join your people everywhere in his song of praise:
"Blessed is the One who comes in the name of the Lord."
Amen.

Good Friday

Isaiah 52:13–53:12; Psalm 22; Hebrews 10:16-25; John 18:1–19:42

On Good Friday, we remember the mourners: the women who followed Jesus, the beloved disciple, the disciples who fled, Jesus' mother. We are with them in their anguish and fear. Those who stayed saw the agony and injustice of death, but they also saw through their tears a victor on the cross, not a victim. They saw the One who died out of love for all the earth. They saw Jesus in his dying hours, still their leader who knew what to do, entrusting his mother to his friend and his friend to his mother so that they would not grieve alone. Jesus' compassion from the cross extended to his executioners and the criminal dying with him who asked for his care. We remember and are silenced by God's grief over the death of an only Son who was sent to save the world God loves. We remember also that the promise of this gift of unbounded love is eternal life, and thus we have courage to follow the small band of mourners through the devastating task of a hasty burial and, after the Sabbath, on the path to the empty tomb.

> He was oppressed, and he was afflicted,
>   yet he did not open his mouth;
> like a lamb that is led to the slaughter,
>   and like a sheep that before its shearers is silent,
>   so he did not open his mouth.
> By a perversion of justice he was taken away.
>   Who could have imagined his future?
>
>   Out of his anguish he shall see light;
> he shall find satisfaction through his knowledge.
>   The righteous one, my servant, shall make many
>   righteous,
>   and he shall bear their iniquities.
>   (Isaiah 53:7-8*b*, 11)

What language shall I borrow to thank thee, dearest
    friend,
    for this thy dying sorrow, thy pity without end?
O make me thine forever; and should I fainting be,
Lord, let me never, never outlive my love to thee.
                ("O Sacred Head, Now Wounded")

Merciful God,
you sent Jesus your Son to die for your love of the world;
you know our grief;
you know the shadow of death that hangs over us.
Turn our faces upward toward the cross,
that we may see the One who poured out himself to death,
now high and lifted up, risen and glorious,
with outstretched arms.
Take us by the hand
and give us voices to sing your praise,
for you will prevail, and death itself will die.
In the name of Jesus, whose victory is life. Amen.

Easter

*Acts 10:34-43; Psalm 118:1-2; 1 Corinthians 15:1-11, 19-26;
Luke 24:1-12*

The Easter story of the empty tomb, with its promise of
final victory, is our sure and steadfast proclamation to the
grieving. "Christ is risen!" This is what we preach at
funerals and what we say to families and friends in
mourning. The trumpet sounds, the feasting, the dancing,
and the laughter of Easter morning may seem far off to
those who have recently lost loved ones, but we know
they will ring true for all of us at God's great resurrection
feast. Until then, we are called to embrace the sorrowing,
assuring them of our oneness as a community who suffers
together and rejoices together. In the Easter communion of
the Eucharist we are asked to taste the broken bread so

that our eyes may be opened and we may recognize our risen Lord. Through the communal reaffirmation of our baptismal covenant, we acknowledge that we have come through the waters of a death like Christ's, and we know that we will one day rise like him. As a community in prayer and praise, we proclaim God's power to bring life out of death. Christ is risen. Christ is risen indeed!

> The powers of death have done their worst,
> but Christ their legions hath dispersed;
> let shouts of holy joy outburst: Alleluia!
>
> Lord, by thy stripes which wounded thee,
> from death's dread sting thy servants free,
> that we may live, and sing to thee: Alleluia!
> ("The Strife Is O'er, the Battle Done," 1695)

God, giver of life,
you raised Jesus from the dead,
the sign of promise for those who have died.
We praise you and give you thanks.
Comfort this day the dying and those who mourn.
Give us grace to be with them in the stillness of their
    shadows;
shelter them beneath your wings.
As Jesus stood again among his friends,
give us courage to stand with those
who are denied what they need for life.
Lead us to your living waters, flowing free;
spread before us your feast of fine food, abundantly
    given.
Teach us the glad shouts and songs of Easter joy,
that we may sing them as our hymn of hope
against the fears that divide us,
for Jesus, by his lifting up, will draw the world to you.
In the name of Jesus Christ, risen indeed. Amen.

Ascension

Acts 1:1-11; Psalm 47; Ephesians 1:15-23; Luke 24:44-53

Jesus' ascension completes his resurrection. In the garden, on Easter morning, Jesus finds Mary Magdalene; in her joy at seeing him alive she wants to hold him there with her. But Jesus was raised to life for the whole world and must be free to take his place again at the right hand of God. Jesus tells Mary, "I am ascending . . . to my God and your God" (John 20:17). The love of God and Jesus for each other will extend to the whole community. Jesus is going to his God and our God and, together with the Spirit, they will create a new household that will be open to all. Poor Lazarus is in this resurrection household, being rocked in Abraham's bosom. The homeless, the outcasts, those who have no access to life are there as well. And in the words of the African American spiritual, "There's plenty good room . . . , —just choose your seat and sit down."

> Then he led them out as far as Bethany, and, lifting up his hands, he blessed them. While he was blessing them, he withdrew from them and was carried up into heaven.
> (Luke 24:50-51)

> See! the heaven its Lord receives, Alleluia!
> Yet he loves the earth he leaves, Alleluia!
> Though returning to his throne, Alleluia!
> Still he calls the world his own, Alleluia!
> ("Hail the Day That Sees Him Rise,"
> Charles Wesley, 1739)

God, ruler of all,
when Jesus was lifted to your throne above,
he blessed his friends below.
Bless us now, O God.
Bless the poor, the meek,
the hungry, the thirsty,

the merciful, the pure in heart,
the peacemakers, those who are persecuted.
And, dear God, bless those who mourn.
Comfort them and hold their loved ones in your care.
Give them hope in Jesus, who calls the world his own.
Bring us to live in your wide circle of love,
that we may be at home at last
where Jesus lives and reigns with you and the Holy Spirit,
now and forever. Amen.

Pentecost

Acts 2:1-21; Psalm 104:24-34, 35b; 1 Corinthians 12:3b-13; John 14:8-17, 25-27

In John's Gospel, the disciples' pain over Jesus' leaving them is palpable. They are grieving, and Jesus, in his tender care for them, tells them repeatedly that he is going to be with his Father and that he will prepare a place for them. But like many who are in grief, the disciples cannot hear far-off promises. They need present assurances; they cry out—as would we—for comfort now. Nobody knows their sorrow and weakness like Jesus, the Word made flesh. So it is Jesus' Spirit, the Advocate or Comforter, who will come and be Jesus' sustaining presence with them. The Spirit will teach them to remember Jesus, enable them to return to their works of ministry, and bring them peace. Memory; action that continues the work of the loved one; and *shalom,* which encompasses healing, wholeness, and peace: these are what the grieving need. Thus the Pentecost feast is a celebration of Jesus' resurrection in our lives now. Through the Spirit's power we can endure and begin the walk of abundant life.

> Nobody knows the trouble I see,
> Nobody knows the trouble I see,
> Nobody knows like Jesus.
> (African American spiritual)

For just as the body is one and has many members, and all the members of the body, though many, are one body, so it is with Christ. For in the one Spirit we were all baptized into one body—Jews or Greeks, slaves or free—and we were all made to drink of one Spirit.

(1 Corinthians 12:12-13)

God, our very present help,
your Son Jesus returned to you
and sent the Comforter, the Spirit of truth, to be near us.
Have mercy on us, O God, and give us peace.
Remember Jesus' promise that we would not be orphaned;
give to the lonely and grieving ones a sure sign of your
    presence.
Grant that your people, united by your Spirit,
may accept each other's sorrows and act in one accord
to be Christ's body that bears the burdens of the world.
Together in Jesus' name, lead us to drink of one Spirit
and share one hope of life in our eternal home,
where Jesus reigns with you and the Spirit,
one God, now and forever. Amen.

Saint Mary Magdalene (July 22)

Ruth 1:6-18; Psalm 73:23-28; 2 Corinthians 5:14-18; John 20:1-2, 11-18

Mary Magdalene was the chief mourner for Jesus, along with his mother and aunt. All four Gospels place her at the cross and burial of Jesus. John says she was "standing near the cross" (John 19:25). We know little else about Mary Magdalene except that she was healed by Jesus and in gratitude supported his ministry financially. She also traveled with him and the Twelve and thus ministered with them (Luke 8:1-3). But we know her primarily for her willingness to stay with her friend Jesus as he was dying, remain for the burial, and return after the Sabbath to anoint the body with spices. She endured the shadow of the cross, not escaping the worst that death can do; she knew death's bitterness. But for that reason she was also the first one at the empty tomb, the first one to meet the risen Jesus, the first one commissioned to tell the others, "He is risen! Let us live!" We tell the Easter story through her eyes. Mary learned of the resurrection when Jesus called her name, and we know that Jesus, raised from the dead and ascended to God's right hand, will call our names too and calls even now the names of those who have gone before us.

> Were you there when they crucified my Lord?
> Were you there when they crucified my Lord?
> Oh! Sometimes it causes me to tremble, tremble, tremble.
> Were you there when they crucified my Lord? . . .
> Were you there when they laid him in the tomb? . . .
> Were you there when he rose up from the grave?
> (African American spiritual)

> Hush. Hush. Somebody's calling my name.
> Hush. Hush. Somebody's calling my name.
> Hush. Hush. Somebody's calling my name.
> Oh my Lord, oh my Lord, what shall I do?

> Sounds like Jesus. Somebody's calling my name.
> Sounds like Jesus. Somebody's calling my name.
> Sounds like Jesus. Somebody's calling my name.
> Oh my Lord, oh my Lord, what shall I do?
> (African American spiritual)

Gracious God, as Jesus restored Mary Magdalene to health
and called her to witness to the resurrection,
may we extend your healing hand to those anguished by
    illness
and offer your word of life to those in despair.
Grant us courage to stay with Mary near the cross,
that we may stand with those unjustly condemned,

give hope and comfort to the dying,
and mourn with those who grieve.
Lift us from our sorrow that we may hear you call our name,
for we will join again the Easter laughter,
and taste the joy of Jesus raised to life.
In the name of Jesus Christ, who rose in glory to be with
you, our God now and forever. Amen.

Saint Michael and All Angels (September 29)

Genesis 28:10-17; Psalm 103; Revelation 12:7-12; John 1:47-51

Michael the archangel does not fit with the modern
image of cosmetically enhanced angels. He is instead a
fierce defender, credited in the book of Daniel with stop-
ping the forces of the chief prince of Persia, and in
Revelation with leading the battle against the dragon,
throwing Satan to earth. In medieval art he appears
often in paintings of Doom, standing guard at death's
gateway with his sword in one hand and a scale for
weighing souls in judgment in the other. But in the Bible
Michael is Israel's protector, and against the great enemy
death, we need such a protector. The collect for Saint
Michael and All Angels in *The Book of Common Prayer*
prays: "Mercifully grant that, as your holy angels always
serve and worship you in heaven, so by your appoint-
ment they may help and defend us here on earth."

Susanna Wesley wrote in her commentary on the
Apostles' Creed that "all saints, as well those on earth as
those in heaven, have communion with God, the Father,
Son, and Holy Ghost; with the blessed angels, who not
only join in devotion with the Church triumphant above,
but are likewise sent forth to minister to those who are the
heirs of salvation while they remain in this world.*

---

* From Susanna Wesley, *Commentary on the Apostles' Creed*, 1670–1742,
as quoted in *For All the Saints: A Prayer Book for and by the Church*, ed.
F. J. Schumacher (Delhi, N.Y.: American Lutheran Publicity Bureau, 1995).

Swing low, sweet chariot, coming for to carry me home;
Swing low, sweet chariot, coming for to carry me home.
I looked over Jordan, and what did I see,
coming for to carry me home?
A band of angels coming after me,
coming for to carry me home.

(African American spiritual)

And flights of angels sing thee to thy rest.

(William Shakespeare)

God of all the heavenly hosts,
when Jacob, far from home, lay down to sleep,
you showed him a stairway filled with angels,
going up and coming down, who led you to his side.
Come to us now in our sadness and need.
Send your angels to find us,
for we are in a strange and desolate land.
Stand beside us as we sleep;
go with us wherever we go and bring us safely home,
that we may join the hosts of heaven
in their song of endless praise to Jesus Christ,
whose birth and rising from the dead
was told by angels' songs.
In the name of this same Jesus,
who reigns with you and the Holy Spirit,
one God, for evermore. Amen.

All Saints Day (November 1)

Isaiah 25:6-9; Psalm 24; Revelation 21:1-6a; Matthew 5:1-12

When we think of the communion of saints, we are likely to
have a picture in mind somewhat like a family portrait. We
may see, seated at the heavenly banquet, a group that includes
the saints we know from the Bible and, intermingled with
them, our loved ones who have died. This is comforting and
truthful, but our banquet table may not have enough leaves in
it. We have Jesus' story of the host who, in order to fill the
table, searches the highways and hedges for the socially unac-
ceptable, the misfits, the sick, and the poor. We have also John's
word in Revelation that God has provided for the healing of
the nations (22:2), so we can expect to dine with former enemies, with all races and families. Expanding the table gives
assurance that all are welcomed, that God shows no partiality.
Furthermore, we already have such communion in the
Eucharist where we recognize the presence at the table of all
God's saints in glory. Through the communion of saints we
have witnesses to the resurrection; we also have an unbroken
circle of relationship with those we love who have died.

> And [God] will destroy on this mountain
>   the shroud that is cast over all peoples,
>   the sheet that is spread over all nations;
> [God] will swallow up death forever.
> Then the Lord God will wipe away the tears from all faces.
>   (Isaiah 25:7-8a)

> On the margin of the river, washing up its silver spray,
> we will walk and worship ever, all the happy golden day.
> Yes, we'll gather at the river, the beautiful, the beautiful
>   river;
> gather with the saints at the river that flows by the
>   throne of God.
>   ("Shall We Gather at the River," Robert Lowry, 1864)

God of all saints,
you have promised that the shroud will be destroyed,
that death will be no more.
While we wait, teach us to sing of hope,
to praise you for your community of love
that embraces us in life and death.
Teach us to pray surrounded by your witnesses,
that we may know the joy of saints who rest in you.
Keep our loved ones in your care
and bring us through the pain of parting,
sure that we will meet again to join the song of life.
O God, you make all things new;
give us newness of life even in this world's shadows
and make us ready to join your blessed communion,
those who shine with you in glory
through Jesus Christ our Lord, now and forever. Amen.

Reign of Christ Sunday

*Ezekiel 34:11-16, 20-24; Psalm 100; Ephesians 1:15-23;
Matthew 25:21-46*

The character of Christ's reign is identified before Jesus'
birth in the song his mother sings: it will be a reign of
reversal where the poor have enough to eat and the rich
have empty stomachs, where the powerful are brought
down and the lowly are lifted up (Luke 1:46-55). Death,
the most powerful enemy of all, will be toppled. We also
know that when the Lamb is on the throne, there will be a
great gathering (Revelation 7:9). Paul describes the mystery of the kingdom this way: "The trumpet will sound,
and the dead will be raised imperishable" (1 Corinthians
15:52).

On the last Sunday of the church year, when in the
Northern Hemisphere the year itself seems to be dying,
we celebrate Christ's reign, already begun and coming in
its fullness in God's own time. Christ's sovereignty

reverses the hold death has over us and lifts us from the
shadows that surround us, for Jesus was exalted to the
throne of glory through his own death and resurrection.

> Jesus the Savior reigns, the God of truth and love;
> When he had purged our stains, he took his seat above.
> Lift up your heart, lift up your voice;
> Rejoice; again I say, rejoice.
>
> Rejoice in glorious hope! Jesus the Judge shall come,
> And take his servants up to their eternal home.
> Lift up your heart, lift up your voice;
> Rejoice; again I say, rejoice.
> ("Rejoice, the Lord Is King," Charles Wesley, 1746)

> King Jesus is a-listening all day long,
>   to hear somebody pray.
>   (African American spiritual)

God, ruler of earth and heaven,
you anointed Jesus to reign with you
where the lowly are raised up
and the hungry have good things.
Give us grace to live justly
and in harmony with all creation.
As Jesus hears the cries of the poor
and weeps with those who mourn,
make us listeners who hear the troubles of the world
and bring your healing touch to the tired and grieving.
Strengthen our love for one another
that we may show in all the earth your new creation.
Teach us to walk today and every day with you
in living hope of your eternal reign,
where the beloved circle of our friends remains unbroken,
and Jesus Christ is Lord of all.
In his name we pray. Amen.

VIII

A Service of Healing

At some point during the time of mourning, the bereaved persons may turn toward a recognition of their need for healing. The biblical admonition to send for the elders of the church and have them pray and anoint points to the tradition of a ritual of anointing or laying on of hands, and prayer (James 5:13-15a). At a healing service, the sorrowing receive the blessings of the community and the recognition that, though the grieving may not be over, God's life-giving power is at work within them.

—⁓—

Greeting

Leader:
"Are any among you suffering? They should pray. Are any cheerful? They should sing songs of praise. Are any among you sick? They should call for the elders of the church and have them pray over them, anointing them with oil in the name of the Lord. The prayer of faith will save the sick and the Lord will raise them up" (James 5:13-15*a*).

We come to this place to be sustained by the communion of Christ's table. We learn together what it is to feast on the mountain and drink from the fountain that never runs dry. From the abundance of God's feast we extend the power of the community's prayer to the sick, the dying, and to those who suffer loss.

Let us pray:

God of peace,
you know our every weakness;
you calm all troubled hearts.
Come to us in your mercy,
that we may be whole in body and mind
and live in harmony with all creation.
In the name of Jesus our healer. Amen.

*(Hymn; suggestions: "O for a Thousand Tongues to Sing,"
"All Creatures of Our God and King")*

Acts of Reconciliation

Leader:
I invite you now to answer God's call to be reconciled to
one another and to God. Let us ask for forgiveness and
make peace. With God's help, let us put aside discord and
conflict and seek God's peace and wholeness.

Let us pray together:

God of mercy,
you hear us when we cry to you.
Touch us now with your healing power.
Help us to lay before you every regret and disappointment;
teach us to live together in love with our neighbors.
Forgive us when we have failed to act for the common good,
and pardon us when we have acted heedlessly or
against your will. Guide our thoughts to your love, that
we may accept your words of peace.
In the name of Jesus, who lifts all earth's peoples to you.
Amen.

(Silent prayers)

Leader:
God, you are faithful and just;
you heal and forgive us.
Lead us to your still waters,
that we may have harmony with each other,
peace within our hearts, and hope for your future.
In Jesus' name. Amen.

Christ is our peace. He breaks down the walls that divide
us, and makes us whole. Let us now exchange greetings
and signs of peace.

(The participants greet each other with handclasps or embraces, exchanging greetings such as "The peace of Christ be with you.")

(Hymn; suggestions: "Dona Nobis Pacem," "Shalom to You")

Prayers for the Sick and Suffering

Leader:
Let us pray now for those in our community whom we know to be sick or suffering. If you know of others, you may stand and speak their names as you wish. After each petition, I will close with the words "Grant our *[sister/brother]* healing and peace. God, in your mercy," and you will respond: **"Hear our prayer."**

Let us pray:

God of compassion,
you look with tender mercy on all who suffer,
and you offer your healing balm to the sick.
Remember those whose names we bring before you;
give them the comfort of your presence
and make them whole again.
Grant our *[sister/brother Name]* healing and peace.
God, in your mercy,
Hear our prayer.

(Silence)

Grant also those we name in our hearts healing and peace.
God, in your mercy,
Hear our prayer.

Hear our prayers, O Lord,
and grant us grace to live in the light of your love.
Through Jesus our Savior, who suffered, died,

and was raised to reign in glory that we might have life.
Amen.

The prayers that bring healing may be the ones we pray
most often. Let us pray the prayer that Jesus taught:

Our Father, who art in heaven,
 hallowed be thy name.
 Thy kingdom come,
 thy will be done on earth as it is in heaven.
Give us this day our daily bread.
And forgive us our trespasses,
 as we forgive those who trespass against us.
And lead us not into temptation,
 but deliver us from evil.
For thine is the kingdom, and the power, and the glory,
forever. Amen.

Invitation to Anointing

Leader:
Please say with me now Psalm 23.

The LORD is my shepherd, I shall not want.
 You make me lie down in green pastures;
 you lead me beside still waters;
  you restore my soul.
 You lead me in right paths
  for your own name's sake.
Even though I walk through the darkest valley,
 I fear no evil;
for you are with me;
 your rod and your staff—
 they comfort me.
You prepare a table before me
 in the presence of my enemies;
you anoint my head with oil;

my cup overflows.
Surely goodness and mercy shall follow me
all the days of my life,
and I shall dwell in the house of the LORD
my whole life long.

(Scripture adaptation)

The act of anointing with oil, a sign of the presence of the Holy Spirit and the care of the community, is available to all who long for the healing touch of God's hand to still our troubled minds and to comfort us in pain and sickness. You are all invited to come forward and kneel in prayer. If you wish, we will anoint you and pray with you.

(The pastor or other pastoral leaders, such as members of the intercessory prayer group, may lay hands on each person's head as she/he prays, and offer to anoint by touching a thumb into the oil and making the sign of the cross on the person's forehead, using these or similar words:)

[Name], I anoint you with oil in the name of Jesus Christ our healer. May the Spirit of the living God be with you. May God bring you wholeness and give you peace. Amen.

Prayer After Anointing

Leader:
Let us pray:

God our Shepherd,
you anointed Jesus to bring us your favor;
grant wholeness to those who are sick
and hope to those who sorrow.
Give them rest in your green fields;
refresh them near calm waters.

Anoint them with healing oil;
revive them with your Spirit.
God, in your mercy,
restore your creation;
bring us to health.
May your justice and love
attend all our days.
Through Jesus, your Son
and our promise of life. Amen.*

*(Hymn; suggestions: "There Is a Balm in Gilead," "Precious
Lord, Take My Hand")*

Dismissal with Blessing

Leader:
Jesus lived among us, healing the sick and teaching us to
love our neighbors. Jesus blessed those who mourned and
comforted his friends in their grief. Let us go in thanksgiving for his great gift of life, refreshed by his Spirit, and
consecrated to his healing purpose.

Let us offer our thanks to God and receive God's blessing:

We thank you, gracious God,
that you formed us in our mother's womb
and remembered us all our days.
God's mercy endures forever.

We thank you, loving God,
that you sent your Son Jesus Christ
to reconcile all people to you.
God's mercy endures forever.

---

* This prayer by the author first appeared in *Liturgy, the Journal of the
Liturgical Conference* (Spring, 1997) 14:1. Used by permission.

We thank you, ever-present God,
that you sent your Holy Spirit
to comfort us and lead us to your truth.
God's mercy endures forever.

We praise you for your healing power
that brings us streams of living water
and gathers us all to your eternal home.
God's name be praised. Amen.

The Lord bless you and keep you.
The Lord's face shine upon you.
The Lord look on you with kindness
and give you peace. Amen.

IX

Linked with the
Sorrow of the World

An individual who is grieving may not be ready for a long time to see her or his sorrow as joined with the sorrow of others. But as a community of faith, we affirm God's love of the whole world, and God's taking on the world's sorrows. The great lament texts of the Old Testament weep over the city and the nation, and as Christ's body, we pray for the healing of the earth. Until God's final destruction of death, we are linked throughout the world in a circle of grief that suffers together and stands together in hope, relying on God's word of life.

—ᴍ—

Prayer for Dying Children in Africa

People were bringing little children to him in order that he might touch them; and the disciples spoke sternly to them. But when Jesus saw this, he was indignant and said to them, "Let the little children come to me; do not stop them; for it is to such as these that the kingdom of God belongs. Truly I tell you, whoever does not receive the kingdom of God as a little child will never enter it." And he took them up in his arms, laid his hands on them, and blessed them.

(Mark 10:13-16)

But when [they] saw the amazing things that he did, and heard the children crying out in the temple, "Hosanna to the Son of David," they became angry and said to him, "Do you hear what these are saying?" Jesus said to them, "Yes; have you never read,
'Out of the mouths of infants and nursing babies
you have prepared praise for yourself'?"

(Matthew 21:15-16)

God our Creator, by your grace
you have blessed the earth with children's voices
singing your praise.
Hear also the cries of children everywhere
whose dying is an affront to your goodness.
We remember especially the children of Africa
whose lives are put at risk by famine and disease.
You, compassionate God, are the Father of consolation,
the Mother of all hope.
Give comfort to those who are orphaned
and those near to death for want of a mother's comfort, a father's tender care.
You, generous God, are the giver of the Bread of life.

Teach us to trust you as our provider
and let go what we do not need,
that your abundant gifts may reach your hungry children.
You, tender God, sent your Son to be our healer,
to bless the children and restore daughters and sons.
Give us his concern for the little ones, those in need of
medicine, doctors, a home, and all that is required for life.
Give us courage to heal in your name,
to offer the resources of our rich nation
for the sake of ending epidemics and starvation.
You, loving God, know our names and call us
through the fire and water to your arms.
Take away the lonely children's fear and despair;
teach us their names that we may keep them always in
    our heart.
You, merciful God, sent Jesus to become a little child,
threatened as a babe by homelessness and by a tyrant's rage.
Give us grace to find in the weakness of a child the power
    for life
that comes as the gift of your Son's death and resurrection.
In Jesus' name, who is our life and peace. Amen.

Prayer for Victims of War

[The LORD] shall judge between many peoples,
    and shall arbitrate between strong nations far away;
they shall beat their swords into plowshares,
    and their spears into pruning hooks;
nation shall not lift up sword against nation,
    neither shall they learn war any more;
but they shall all sit under their own vines and under
their own fig trees,
    and no one shall make them afraid;
    for the mouth of the LORD of hosts has spoken.
                                        (Micah 4:3-4)

God of all the nations,
you have broken down the dividing wall of hostility
and called us all to be reconciled to one another.
Free us from fear and doubts,
that we may praise you by our lives of peace.
Give us courage to look beyond the terror of deception
    and pride,
that we may see your wonders of goodness and grace.
Bless those who are victims of their nations' warring
    madness,
whose lives are endangered by open conflict and who live
    in dread.
Embrace those who are dying in the streets from bombs
    and snipers;
be with those whose farms are turned to battlefields
    and whose homes are destroyed.
Hold in your arms those who die in innocence and
    forgive those who die from their own actions,
for in life and death we are your children, dependent
    on your care.
Unite us by your Spirit of truth
that we may put aside all greed and selfishness.
Lead us to be ambassadors of your peace,
that all people may enjoy the shade of their own trees
and live in fear no more.
Teach us, God, to look to the Lord of life,
who by his death and resurrection lifts us to your love.
In the name of Jesus, Lord and Savior. Amen.

Prayer for Victims of Violent Crimes

Do not fear, for I am with you,
  do not be afraid, for I am your God;
I will strengthen you, I will help you,
  I will uphold you with my victorious right hand.

(Isaiah 41:10)

God, sorrowing Parent and just Judge of all,
Hear us now, for we are in anguish;
terrors fall on us and horror overwhelms us.
Give us wings to fly from the flood of grief and pain,
from the cold wind of hate and the scorching heat of
  anger.
Free us from the hands that deal violence on the earth.
We are worn out with our weeping;
our throats are parched,
for we cry out to you in the evening, in the morning, and
  at noon.
At an acceptable time, O God,
in the abundance of your steadfast love, answer us.

God of mercy,
you are with your children at the moment of death.
In the shattering fury or the quiet fading of breath,
the light of your face shines on them.
Hold in your sight those we can no longer see.
Keep in your everlasting arms
those cut down and taken from us in senseless acts of
  rage.
Be to us a rock of refuge,
a sanctuary from the evil that defies your will.
Your Son Jesus Christ died a violent death,

and you raised him to be the resurrection and the life:
Send us your mercy and open to us the way to life.
In Jesus' name. Amen.

(from Psalms 55, 58, 61, 69, 71)

Prayer for the Condemned

Out of the depths I cry to you, O LORD.
　　Lord, hear my voice!
Let your ears be attentive
　　to the voice of my supplications!
If you, O LORD, should mark iniquities,
　　Lord, who could stand?
But there is forgiveness with you,
　　so that you may be revered.
I wait for the LORD, my soul waits,
　　and in his word I hope;
my soul waits for the Lord
　　more than those who watch for the morning,
　　more than those who watch for the morning.

(Psalm 130:1-6)

God, our Judge and Ruler,
your mercy rains down on the just and on the unjust.
Wash with your mercy those who have been condemned
　　to die.
Search for them as you sought the son who went to a far
　　country.
Speak of your redeeming love to them in their anguish,
hear their cries of regret and fear.
Show them even as they wait for death a gateway to
　　your goodness.
Show them your tears of sorrow, shed for them
and for those whose lives were shattered by their acts.

Have mercy on us who wait for justice, and calm our
    fears.
Keep all lives safe from violence,
and teach us to guard against perversions of justice.
You alone know the secrets of our hearts:
Give us strength and patience
that we may yield to you our longing for vengeance.
We know that all have fallen short of your glory:
Forgive our sins and move us to forgive others.
Grant to our leaders human kindness, to our courts
    wisdom,
and to our nation compassion.
Give us regard for the needy, the desperate, the lonely,
    the sick,
and give us strength to stand with all creation,
singing the song of life against all the threats of death.
In the name of our Redeemer, who lives and conquers
    death for all. Amen.

Prayer for Creation

I consider that the sufferings of this present time are not worth comparing with the glory about to be revealed to us. For the creation waits with eager longing for the revealing of the children of God; for the creation was subjected to futility, not of its own will but by the will of the one who subjected it, in hope that the creation itself will be set free from its bondage to decay and will obtain the freedom of the glory of the children of God. We know that the whole creation has been groaning in labor pains until now; and not only the creation, but we ourselves, who have the first fruits of the Spirit, groan inwardly while we wait for adoption, the redemption of our bodies. For in hope we were saved. Now hope that is seen is not hope. For who hopes for what is seen? But if we hope for what we do not see, we wait for it with patience.

(Romans 8:18-25)

God of the earth and sky,
your breath swept over the water at creation;
your word brought forth light and swarms of living
   creatures.
Give us grace to live wisely in the home you have created,
that we may manage well
and not destroy what you have made.
God of beauty, you clothe the lilies;
you hold the sparrows in your hand.
Teach us your tender care of all things living,
both small and great,
that we may live in harmony with the music of the
   spheres.
Teach us to preserve the earth, the work of your hands,
for us and for our descendants,

to honor the glory of your name.
Open our eyes to the carelessness that threatens earth's
    integrity;
let us hear the groaning of creation for your saving grace.
You have taken us as your children, God;
now fill us with the Spirit's glory
that we may join the circle of your love
and live in communion with earth and all its creatures,
waiting for the day when death will end and weeping
    will be no more.
In the name of Jesus, the bright and morning star. Amen.

Postscript

Prayer in the Time of Trial

A Postscript Written Following September 11, 2001

On September 11, 2001, I with millions of other television viewers watched as the second plane hit the World Trade Center towers. Within seconds, a familiar landmark, a place where tourists and office workers were gathering for the day, became a place of horror. We were watching in "real time" as hundreds of people died violently. Few of us moved from our television sets in the next hour, and when the towers collapsed in a cloud of smoke and ash, we knew the number of the dead would be thousands.

Recovery from the shock of that moment has hardly begun. We were overwhelmed by the reality that we had watched evil shatter lives in a single instant. We were astounded when we learned that suicide hijackers were responsible for this unthinkable act of using passenger planes to slam into buildings. It seemed beyond imagination that one person could be persuaded to bring about the violent destruction of his own life and the lives of so many people who were unknown to him, much less that nineteen young men, some with families, had prepared for months to do so. We seemed further than ever from the promised day when swords will become plowshares. We had, in fact, experienced the reverse: an ordinary means of going about everyday business was turned into an instrument of war.

The response to this event has also been astonishing. Places of worship were filled to overflowing for special memorial services and for regularly scheduled services during the weeks following the attack. In a modern, secular society, always driven by the need to get on with things, it is a rare sight to encounter so many people praying. Prayer of course was known as a healing agent in biblical times and has, after much research, been recognized as such even by contemporary medical scientists. But following the terrorist attacks, those who pray regularly and those who had not felt the need to pray for a long time cried with Paul, that we do not know how to pray as we ought, asking the Spirit to intercede for us "with sighs too deep for words" (Romans 8:26).

Its healing power is not the only thing that draws people to prayer in times of disaster. Through prayer we give over to God those who are suffering and dying. God told Moses from the burning bush, "I have observed the misery of my people; . . . I know their sufferings, and I have come down to deliver them" (Exodus 3:7-8). God is always found among the suffering people. And though we do not claim to know all that happens in death, we know this: All creation is held in God's hand, and nothing, not even death itself, separates us from God's love (Romans 8:38-39).

Prayer also works in and through us as an agent for change. Prayer, rather than being a passive activity or a numbing solace, wakes us up from the deep sleep our grief has brought on us and prepares us to face even the unthinkable. Jesus on the Mount of Olives, on the night before his passion, wanted, needed, his disciples to pray with him, but they were asleep: "He came to the disciples and found them sleeping because of grief, and he said to them, 'Why are you sleeping? Get up and pray that you may not come into the time of trial' " (Luke 22:45-46). Prayer calls us to be vigilant in the time of trial.

Prayer even allows us to turn our desire for revenge over to God. Prayer allows us to say to God whatever we want to say about our enemies, to cry out against them, and to ask for their destruction. Then, if we pray biblically, surrounded by God's great cloud of witnesses, prayer can change us, turning us into lovers of our enemies, doers of good in the face of evil, desirers of life.

And prayer works among us as a force for forming community. We pray with the resurrection community, the communion of saints, and because we pray that the power of the resurrection may come upon us and cause us to stand up in the midst of suffering, prayer makes us into an anti-death community. We stand up in the face of bio-terrorism, the turning of a life science into an instrument of death. We stand up against the misuse of technology as a threat to our security. We stand up against oppression and injustice that turns human beings into servants of death in all its forms. God gave Jesus to save the world through his suffering, death, and resurrection, and we pray together that we, like Jesus, may serve God's saving purpose, working always for God's will for life.

The events of September 11, 2001, brought us into a worldwide circle of grief. We stand with people everywhere and pray for life. We pray that our lives may become a living worship and that God's truth may triumph through us. The prayers that follow express our longing to be healed from our grief and shock, and voice our faith in God's resurrection power. I hope that they will find a place in memorial services—possibly those planned for the anniversary of the attacks—or for other occasions of remembrance with the grieving.

Prayer for the Victims of the Terrorist Attacks

September 11, 2001

The eternal God is your dwelling place,
and underneath are the everlasting arms.
(Deuteronomy 33:27)

God of the suffering,
you know the misery of your people.
Hear our cry against evil's horror,
against the blows of death and destruction.
Hear us, for we are angry and overwhelmed;
heal us, and calm the tumult of our heart.

Heal us, merciful God.

God of the dying, nothing can separate us from your love.
Give the strength of your arms in the moment of death;
give the light of your face to those who have died.
Hear us, for we fear for those cut off from life;
give them rest and peace now and forever.

Give us peace, merciful God.

God of the grieving,
you seek good for all creation.
Guide our thoughts when we cannot comprehend;
fix our minds on you that we may not lose hope.
Hear us, for we are shattered by the loss of treasured
    lives;
comfort us, compassionate Father, consoling Mother.

Comfort us, merciful God.

God of the living,
you have asked us to choose life,
though all around us seems in the thrall of death.
Send us your resurrection power and make us whole.
Hear us, for we are thirsty and tired;
bring us to the river of life where we may sing again your
    praise.

In Jesus' name. Amen.

Intercessory Prayer*

(Isaiah 43:1-3; Ephesians 11:1-21; Luke 6:20-31)

God of all the ages, you have offered us the immeasurable greatness of your power, which you put to work in Christ when you raised him from the dead and seated him at your right hand. Help us in our distress that we may, by your power, fear neither war's alarms nor deadly pestilence. Enlighten our hearts that we may know the hope to which you have called us.

You have promised that the shroud of death will be destroyed, that weeping will be no more. Hear the cries of those who lost mothers and fathers, husbands and wives, sisters and brothers, colleagues and friends, in the hijacked planes and in the attacks on the World Trade Center and on the Pentagon. Hold them in your arms and surround them with the love of friends. Care for the victims of the violence in Afghanistan, those killed by bombing, and those abused by conflict and oppression. Shelter all refugees beneath your wings and teach us to care for them.

---

* This prayer by Blair Meeks first appeared on the Cokesbury Crisis Response website, www.cokesbury.com, during the week preceding November 4, 2001. Copyright © 2001.

Give help and comfort to the families of the dead and keep us mindful of their anguish. Comfort those in our congregation who are separated by death from those they love. You have promised that the fire will not destroy us and the water will not overwhelm us. Now keep those who have died in your care and bring us through the pain of parting, sure that we are embraced in all things by your love. You have called us by name and redeemed us. Now keep alive in us the memory of those who have died, those we name aloud and those we name in our hearts. *[Names may be read.]*

Your Son Jesus taught us to love our enemies, do good to those who hate us, and bless those who curse us; teach us now to pray for our enemies, those who are visible to us and those who are in hiding. Give us the patience to act only for your justice, the willingness to do good in the face of evil, the kindness to offer your comfort to a hurting world, and the faith to speak your word in all places.

Guide our leaders—the president and his advisers; the Congress; the Supreme Court; governors; and mayors—in their decisions. Give wisdom to our doctors, health workers, and public officials that they may take strong measures against the diseases that threaten us. Give courage, understanding, and constraint to our military officers. Guard the men and women in military service; protect their families and ease their fears.

Gather us now around your table as a community of your faithful people from all ages and nations. Unite us by your Spirit with all the saints. Make us ready to hear your melody of peace, calling us to gather at the river that flows from your throne, and inviting us to worship you forever. In the name of Jesus, whose name is above every name that is named, not only in this age but also in the age to come. Amen.

A Prayer Adapted from Psalms 143 and 79

Hear our prayer, O Lord,
for you are faithful and righteous.
We cry to you: do not judge us,
for we have been crushed.
We remember the days of old
when our cities were secure, our future assured.
We recall all the wonders you have done;
we celebrate the work of your hands.
We reach out to you;
we thirst for you like a parched land.
Answer us quickly, O Lord;
our spirit fails.
Do not hide your face from us,
or we shall be like those who live with death.
Let us hear of your steadfast love in the morning,
for in you we put our trust.
Teach us the way we should go,
for we offer you ourselves.
Save us from our enemies and forgive our sins,
for you are our refuge.
Teach us to do your will,
for you are our God.
Let your good Spirit lead us on a level path,
for the glory of your name.
Send your love speedily to welcome us,
for we are brought very low.
Help us, O God of our salvation,
for the glory of your name.
O Lord, preserve our life, bring us out of trouble
for your name's sake.
Do not remember the sins of our ancestors,
for we are your servants.

And we, your own people, the flock of your pasture,
will give you unending thanks.
From generation to generation
we will sing your praise. Amen.

Kyrie

God our loving Parent,
you grieved for your Son.
Now grieve with us for your children who have died.

Lord, have mercy.
Christ, have mercy.

God our Comforter,
you call the weary and the burdened to your side.
Hear our anguish; heal our wounded hearts.

Lord, have mercy.
Christ, have mercy.

God our Savior,
you are always near at hand.
Save us from the fear of death.

Lord, have mercy.
Christ, have mercy.

God our Shepherd,
you lead us to still waters.
Give rest to us and to those who have died.

Lord, have mercy.
Christ, have mercy.

God our Peace,
you brought back from the dead our Lord Jesus.
Bring us from the shadows of despair.

Lord, have mercy.
Christ, have mercy.

God our only Joy,
your reign will turn our mourning to laughter.
Bring all the earth into your dance of life.

Lord, have mercy.
Christ, have mercy. Amen.

Blessing

Merciful God,
you are with us in times of destruction and evil; even in
the shadow of death, you are there.
Gather us beneath your wings and teach us to sing your
praise.
Keep us, Lord, throughout our life, at our end, and at our
departing.
Look on us with kindness and give us the deep peace of
Christ. Amen.

May the God of hope fill you with all joy and peace in
believing,
so that you may abound in hope
by the power of the Holy Spirit (Romans 15:13).

Amen.